HANDS-ON SCIENCE

TRANSPORT

40 GREAT SCIENCE EXPERIMENTS AND PROJECTS

Consulting editor Chris Oxlade

southwater

This edition is published by Southwater

Southwater is an imprint of Anness Publishing Ltd
Hermes House, 88–89 Blackfriars Road, London SE1 8HA
tel. 020 7401 2077; fax 020 7633 9499
www.southwaterbooks.com; info@anness.com

This edition distributed in the UK by
The Manning Partnership Ltd
tel. 01225 478 444; fax 01225 478 440
sales@manning-partnership.co.uk

This edition distributed in the USA and Canada by
National Book Network
tel. 301 459 3366; fax 301 459 1705
www.nbnbooks.com

This edition distributed in Australia by
Pan Macmillan Australia
tel. 1300 135 113; fax 1300 135 103
customer.service@macmillan.com.au

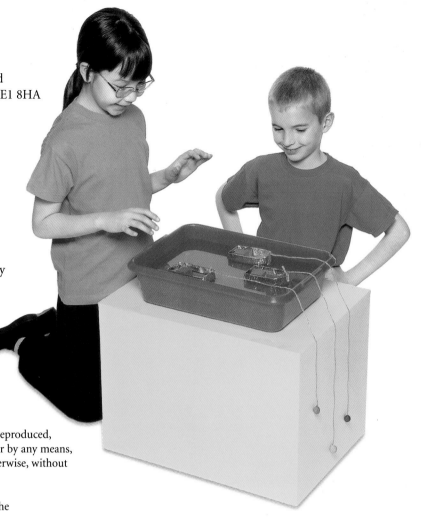

A CIP catalogue record for this book is available from the
British Library.

Publisher: Joanna Lorenz
Managing Editor: Linda Fraser
Editor: Clare Gooden
Production Controller: Darren Price
Contributing Authors: John Farndon, Jen Green, Robin Kerrod, Chris Oxlade,
Steve Parker, Rodney Walshaw
Designer: Axis Design Editions Ltd
Jacket Design: Dean Price
Photographers: Paul Bricknell, John Freeman, Don Last, Robert Pickett, Tim Ridley
Illustrators: Cy Baker/Wildlife Art, Stephen Bennington, Peter Bull Art Studio, Stuart Carter,
Simon Gurr, Richard Hawke, Nick Hawken, Michael Lamb, Alan Male/Linden Artists,
Guy Smith, Clive Spong, Stephen Sweet/Simon Girling and Associates, Alisa Tingley,
John Whetton
Stylists: Ken Campbell, Jane Coney, Marion Elliot, Tim Grabham, Thomasina Smith,
Isolde Sommerfeldt, Melanie Williams

Previously published as part of a larger compendium, *150 Great Science Experiments*.

10 9 8 7 6 5 4 3 2 1

Publisher's Note
The publishers have made every effort to ensure that all instructions
contained within this book are accurate and safe, and cannot accept
liability for any resulting injury, damage or loss to persons or property
however they may arise.

Contents

Travel and Transport

The most powerful, luxurious and specialized forms of transport today all evolved from simple scientific principles. The trick of keeping a luxury passenger liner or a massive oil tanker afloat is basically the same as it was for early humans with their canoes and coracles. Many of the secrets of super-powered vehicles are the result of learning to make use of simple forces such as jet propulsion, thrust, and lift, and combining them with other inventions and new materials. On the following pages, you will discover how boats, trains, cars, planes and spacecraft work by experimenting with the forces that make them go.

Simple boats

Some of the earliest and simplest types of boat are still made today. Small reed boats are still built in southern Iraq and on Lake Titicaca in South America in a similar way to the one in the project below. Reed boats are made by tying thousands of river reeds together into huge bundles. The bundles are then tied together to make hull shapes. In ancient Egypt, large boats were made like this, from papyrus reeds. Some historians believe that Egyptians may have made long ocean crossings in papyrus craft.

The model in the second project is of a coracle. This is a round boat made by covering a light wooden frame with animal hides. Coracles are also still made, but are now covered with canvas treated with tar instead of animal hide. Coracles were small enough for one person to paddle along a river and were used for fishing. When you are out near a river or lake, take photographs or make drawings of other simple craft, such as canoes and punts. See if you can make working models of them, too.

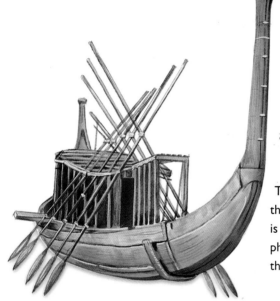

◄ **Afterlife evidence**
This boat was found in a pit alongside the Great Pyramid of Egypt in 1954. It is believed to have been used as a pharaoh's funeral boat, which ferried the dead pharaoh to the afterlife.

Make a reed craft

1 Make bundles of raffia by tying a few dozen strands together with a short piece of raffia. You will need two bundles about 8in long and two more about 10in long.

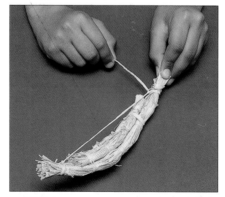

2 Tie the two long bundles and the two short bundles together. Tie the short bundles on top of the long ones. Fix a strand between each end, to make the ends bend up.

3 Gently lower the reed boat onto the surface of a tank of water. How well does it float? Does it stay upright? Try leaving it in the water to see if it becomes waterlogged.

Make a coracle

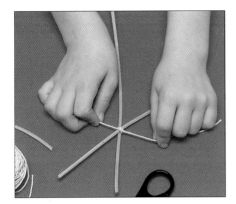

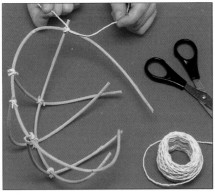

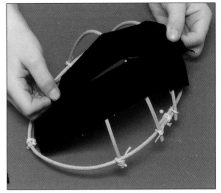

1 Cut one long piece of cane and three short pieces. Using short pieces of string, tie all three of the short pieces of cane to the long piece to make a triple-armed cross.

2 Cut a much longer piece of cane. Form it into a loop, and tie it to all the ends of the triple cross shape. Bend the ends of the cross up as you tie them to form a dish shape.

3 Cut pieces of cotton cloth about 6 x 2in. Apply glue to the outside of the frame, and place the pieces over it. Glue the pieces to each other where they overlap.

4 Glue down the cloth where it folds over the top of the frame. Put two coats of glue on the outside of the cloth to waterproof it. Leave the glue to dry completely.

When the model is dry, put the finished coracle into a tank of water. How well does it float? Why not try making a person from modeling material to sit in your model coracle?

Early Britons used coracles 9,000 years ago. Coracles are light to carry, easy to use, and stable enough to fish from.

Sail power

When you launch your model sailboat, you can get an idea of how it is propelled by the wind. To sail in the direction they want to go, sailors must be aware of wind direction, so that they can adjust the position of the sails to make best use of it. If sailboats face straight into the wind, the sails flap uselessly, and the boat is in a "no-go zone." They can, however, sail into oncoming wind by taking a zigzag course. This is called tacking. The wind blows against one side of the sail to propel the boat diagonally upwind. When the boat changes tack, the wind blows against the other side of the sail, and the boat goes forward on the opposite diagonal. If the wind is blowing from behind the boat, the sail is set at right angles to the boat like an open wing, so that it is filled by the wind.

YOU WILL NEED

pencil, ruler, thick card, scissors, tape, plastic sheet, stapler, bradawl, nonhardening modeling material, thin garden canes, colored paper, plastic straw, small plastic bottle, string, paper clip, sheet of paper.

▲ **Parts of a sailboat**

Sailboats usually have a crew of two people. A helmsman operates the tiller and the mainsail, and a crew works the jib and centerboard (which stops the boat from drifting sideways).

Template ▶

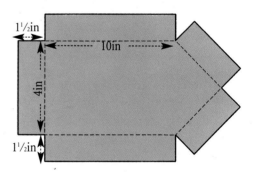

Make a sailboat

1 Cut out your hull shape from thick card, using the template above as a guide. Score along the dotted lines with the scissors. Use tape to fasten the sides together.

2 Lay the hull on a plastic sheet. Cut the plastic around the hull, allowing enough to cover the sides and overlap them at the top by 2in. Fold the sheet over the hull and staple it in place.

3 Pierce a hole in the middle of a strip of card a little wider than the hull. Staple in place. Put modeling material under the hole, and push a 12in cane through the hole into it.

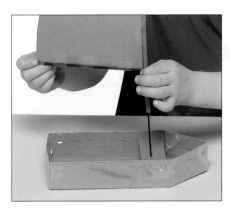

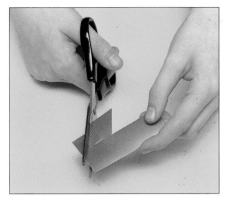

4 Cut a sail from colored paper with a base of about 8in. Attach the straw along the side and a garden cane along the bottom with tape. Slip the straw over the mast.

5 Cut an L-shape (about 3in long, 1½in wide at the base and ¾in wide at the top) from the small plastic bottle. Cut the base of the L in half to make two slanted tabs, as shown.

6 Fold back the two tabs of the L-shaped plastic in opposite directions, as shown, and staple them to the stern (back) of the boat. This is the boat's rudder.

7 Cut a piece of string about 8in long. Tape one end to the back of the boom (the cane), and feed the other end through a paper clip attached to the back of the boat.

8 To test out how your sailboat works, make a breeze by waving a large sheet of paper near to the boat. Adjust the string to move the sail into the right position.

When you have finished your boat, you could try making and adding a centerboard. Attach a cardboard oblong at right angles to the bottom of the boat. It will stop your boat from drifting sideways in the wind.

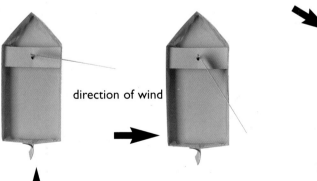

direction of wind

When you test your boat, set the sail in these different positions. Alter the position of the sail by using the string taped to the boom (cane). Follow the arrows shown here to see which way the wind should be blowing from in each case. Try blowing from other directions to see if this makes a difference to your boat.

How ships float

Objects will float if they are less dense (lighter) than water. The water pushes upwards with a force called upthrust. So a light wooden raft will float, but a metal ship must contain enough air to make is overall density less than that of water. The first experiment shows that an object will float if the upthrust of the water is great enough to overcome the downward push of the object's weight. The size of the upthrust depends on how much water the object pushes out of the way. When you put an object in water and let it go, it settles into the water, pushing liquid out of the way. The farther it goes in, the more water it pushes away and the more upthrust acts on it. When the upthrust becomes the same as the object's weight, the object floats.

The second project shows you a hollow hull. If you push a light, hollow ball under water, it will spring back up. Upthrust from the water makes a hollow hull float in the same way. The higher the density of water, the greater the upthrust. This means that ships float slightly higher in salt water, since it is more dense than fresh water.

salt water

fresh water

▲ Measuring density
The density of water is measured with a hydrometer. You can make one by putting a lump of modeling material on the end of a straw. Put it in a glass of water, and mark the water level with tape. Now put the straw in an equal amount of salty water. What happens?

Testing upthrust

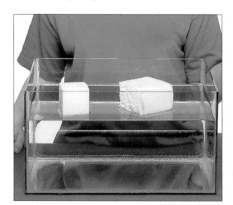

1 Put the two styrofoam chunks into a large tank of water. They will float well, because their material is so light. Only a small amount of upthrust is needed.

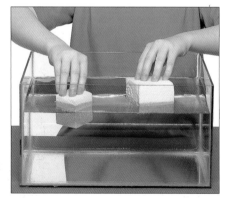

2 Try pushing the chunks under the water. Now you are pushing lots of water aside. Can you feel upthrust pushing back? The bigger chunk will experience more upthrust.

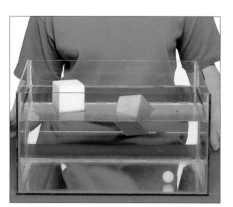

3 A wooden block floats deeper in the water, because wood is more dense (heavier) than styrofoam. A marble sinks, because the upthrust on it is not as great as its weight.

Hollow hulls

1 Put a piece of foil about 8in by 6in into a tank of water. With just the slightest push, it will sink. This is because it does not displace much water, so there is very little upthrust.

2 Lift the sheet of foil out of the water, and dry it carefully with a paper towel. Now mold it into a simple boat shape with your fingers. Take care not to tear the foil.

3 Put your foil boat into the water. It should now float. It will not sink so easily. Its shape pushes aside much more water than it did when it was flat, so the upthrust is greater.

Try filling your foil boat with small objects, such as marbles, for cargo. As you put more marbles in, it will float lower and lower. How many marbles can your boat hold before it sinks?

This simple foil boat works like a real ship's hull. Even though it is made of metal, it is filled with air. This gives the hull shape a much lower overall density.

What's in a hull?

Whenever an object such as a ship moves through the water, the water slows it down. The push made by the water is called water resistance, or drag. The faster the object moves, the greater the water resistance becomes.

If you look around a busy harbor, you will see dozens of different hull designs. Sleek, narrow hulls with sharp bows cause less resistance than wide hulls with square bows, so they can move through the water faster.

You can test how the shape of a bow affects the speed of a ship in this experiment. The deeper a hull sits in the water, the more resistance there is. Some hulls are designed to sit just on top of the water. For example, a small speedboat has a flaring, shallow V-shaped hull designed to skim across the surface. A cargo ship has a square hull that sits lower in the water. Speed is not as important for the cargo ship as it is for the speedboat. Instead, the cargo ship is designed for stability, and to carry as much as possible.

YOU WILL NEED

ruler, pen or pencil, colored stiff card, scissors, tape, aluminum foil, three paper clips, nonhardening modeling material, food scale, string, large plastic bowl, watering can, three equal-sized wooden bricks.

Testing hull shapes

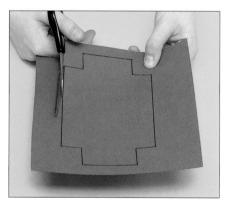

I Use a ruler to draw the three templates shown left on sheets of stiff card. Make sure the corners are square and the edges straight. Carefully cut out the shapes.

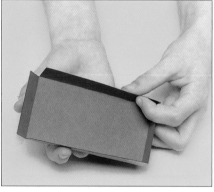

2 Using scissors, score along the lines inside the base of the square boat (shown as dotted lines left). Bend up the sides, and use tape to fix the corners together.

▲ Templates
Use these three templates to help you cut out and make the three boat shapes in this project.

1¼in

1¼in

6in

6in

6in

1¼in

4in

1¼in

6in

4in

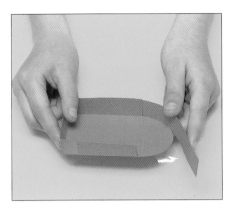

3 Make the round-ended and pointed boats in the same way as the first boat. Use a separate piece of card to make the round bow, and tape it to the base in several places.

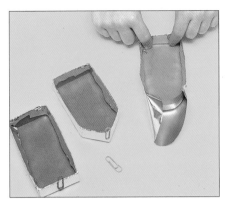

4 Now cover the outside of each shape with foil, neatly folding the foil over the sides. This will make the shapes more waterproof. Fix a paper clip to the bow (front) of each boat.

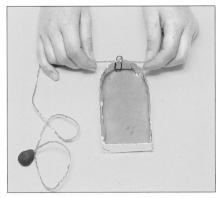

5 Roll out three balls of modeling material about the size of a walnut. Weigh the balls to make sure they are the same weight. Attach a ball to the bow of each boat with string.

6 Put a large plastic bowl on a table or a strong box. Use a watering can to pour water into the trough. The water should be about ½in from the top of the bowl.

Release the boats all at the same time. The weighted strings will pull them along down the length of the bowl. Which one wins the race to the other end of the bowl? Try timing the boats with a stopwatch to work out the difference between the fastest and slowest.

7 Line up the boats at one end of the bowl. Hang the strings and modeling material balls down over the other end. Put a small wooden brick inside each boat.

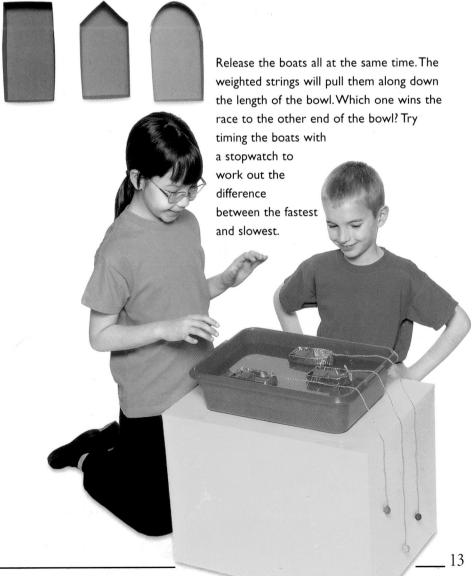

Ship stability

Many ships look as though they are top-heavy, so how do they manage to stay upright and not capsize? These projects will help you understand why. It partly depends on the shape of the hull. If the ship has a wide, flat hull, then when it tips to one side, that side sinks lower into the water. This pushes aside more water, causing more upthrust, which pushes the ship upright again. A round hull will be the same shape in the water when it tips, so it is less stable. A catamaran like the one in the project has two hulls side by side, so its overall shape is very wide, making it extra stable.

The position of the cargo in the hull of the ship is important. Heavy cargo high up on deck makes the ship top-heavy and more likely to tip over. Heavy cargo low down in the hull gives the ship stability. Cargo that can move is dangerous, because it could slip to one side of the ship, causing it to tip suddenly. You will be able to test the effects of different weights in square and rounded hulls in the second experiment.

Make a catamaran

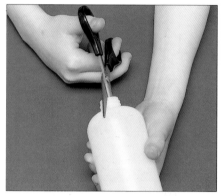

I Remove the top from a small plastic bottle, and carefully cut the bottle in half lengthways. This will leave you with two identical shapes to form the catamaran hulls.

Put your completed catamaran into a tank or bowl of water. Load the hulls with cargo such as wooden bricks. Can you make your boat capsize?

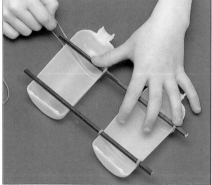

2 Place the two halves of the bottle side by side. Lay two medium-length pieces of garden cane on top. Securely fasten the canes to the bottle halves using rubber bands.

Loading cargo

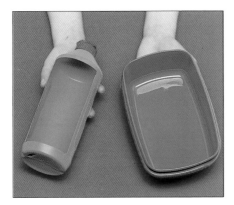

1 For this project, you need one container with a round hull shape and another about the same size with a square hull shape. Cut a strip from the round container to make a hold.

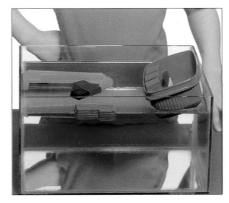

2 Put both containers in a tank or bowl of water. Gradually load one side of each hull with wooden bricks. Which hull capsizes first? Which hull is more stable?

3 Now load the square hull evenly with wooden bricks. You should be able to get a lot more in. Press down on one side of the hull. Can you feel the hull trying to stabilize itself?

4 To stabilize the round hull, press some lumps of modeling material into the bottom of the hull. This adds weight, known as ballast, to the bottom of the hull.

Reload the round hull with wooden bricks. Can you see how the modeling material ballast low down in the hull has made the craft more stable?

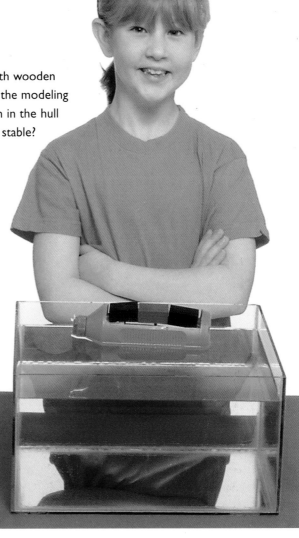

unstable round hull

stable square hull

When a round hull tips to one side, there is little change to the amount of hull underwater. This makes the shape unstable. When a square hull tips to one side, there is a great change in the amount of hull underwater on that side. This makes it stable.

Power and steering afloat

The model boat in this project is fitted with two basic devices for controlling water craft. Both operate underwater. The propeller is driven by the engine of a motor- or steam-powered boat. It rotates very fast and pushes the craft through the water. In the project, the engine power comes from the energy stored in a wound-up rubber band. As in real life propellers, the blades are set at different angles, and push the water backward, so thrusting the vessel forward, as it spins. You could try making different propeller designs—with more blades set at different angles, for example—and testing them to see which works best.

A rudder is used to steer both sail- and motor-powered boats. It is controlled by a handle called a tiller, or a wheel, on the boat. As in your model boat, the rudder can be moved to different positions to make the boat turn left or right, but will only work when the boat is actually moving. In addition to making the boat turn left and right, the rudder also keeps the boat going in a straight line when it is set straight.

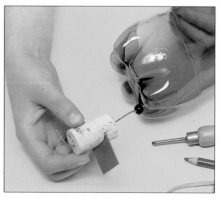

▲ Making a connection
In a large cruise yacht, the rudder is moved by wires linked to the wheel in the cockpit. The wheel drives the sprocket, which moves a chain. Wires attached to the chain move the rudder via pulleys. The yacht is also equipped with a diesel engine that is connected to a single propeller via a driveshaft.

YOU WILL NEED

cork, bradawl, scissors, small plastic bottle, large plastic bottle, large paper clip, pliers (optional), ruler, bead, long rubber bands, small pencil, pool, thin garden cane.

Make a powered boat

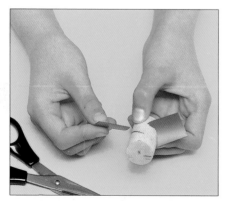

1 Make a hole through the middle of the cork using a bradawl. Cut a diagonal slot in either side of the cork. Push two strips of plastic cut from a small bottle into the slots.

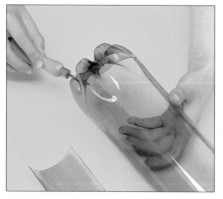

2 Cut an oblong strip from one side of the large plastic bottle. This slot is the top of your boat. With the bradawl, make a small hole at the back of your bottle in the bottom.

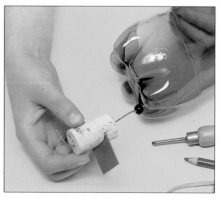

3 Straighten a large paper clip (you may need pliers). Bend the last ½in of wire at right angles. Push the wire through the cork, and thread it through the bead and small hole.

4 Bend the end of the wire inside the bottle. Hook a rubber band over the wire, and stretch it up through the neck of the bottle. Secure it in place with a pencil.

5 To wind up the band, turn the pencil as you hold on to the propeller. Keep holding the propeller until you put the boat into the water and release it. What happens?

6 Now make a rudder for your boat. Cut a piece of plastic about 1½ x 1½in and pierce two holes near one edge. Push a piece of thin cane through the two holes.

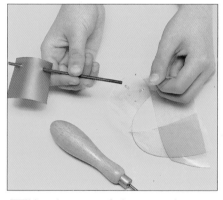

7 Use the strip of plastic cut from the large bottle to support your rudder. Pierce two holes about ¾in apart in the center of the strip, and push the cane through them.

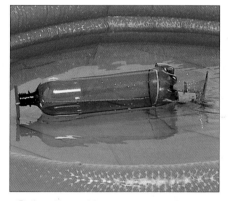

8 Fix the rudder support to the bottle with a rubber band, so that the rudder is clear of the propeller. Wind up the pencil, and put your boat back in the water.

Like a real boat builder, you will want to test the controls of your boat. To do this, start with the rudder centered to make the boat go straight. Next, try turning the rudder from side to side. What happens? How tight a circle can you make your boat turn in?

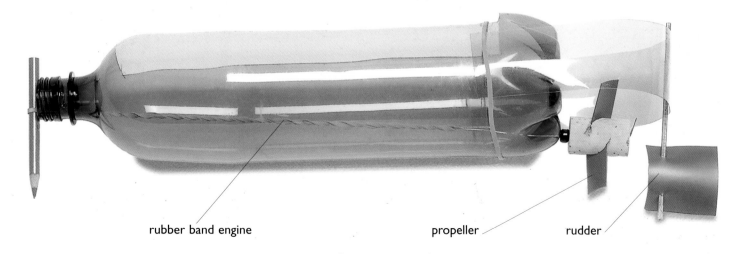

rubber band engine   propeller   rudder

Safety at sea

There are various ways in which ships can be designed to keep afloat. All ships have bilge pumps that pump out water that has collected in the bottom of the hull and expel it into the sea or river. Many sailboats and canoes are fitted with bags of air or styrofoam bricks inside to keep them buoyant (afloat). Most lifeboats are self-righting, which means that they bob back upright if they capsize, like the model in the first project. Self-righting lifeboats are completely watertight—even the air inlets in inflatable lifeboats have seals to keep out water. Heavy engines are set low down, and the hull and high cabins are full of air. This arrangement makes the lifeboat flip upright automatically.

The second and third projects show how hydrofoils and hovercrafts work. These are fast boats, designed for short sea crossings. A hydrofoil is the fastest type of ferry. Under the hull, there are winglike foils. Water flows faster over the foil's curved upper surface than it does over the flat lower surface, creating lift. When traveling at high speed, the foils lift the hull clear of the water.

Try the third project to see how hovercrafts skim across the water supported on cushions of air. Buoyancy tanks stop the hovercraft from sinking if the air cushion fails.

YOU WILL NEED

pencil, ruler, strofoam tile, scissors, nonhardening modeling material, rubber bands, tank or bowl of water, small plastic tub.

Self-righting boat

1 Cut a boat shape about 6 x 4in from styrofoam. Attach a golf-ball sized lump of modeling material to one side of your boat shape with a rubber band.

2 Put your boat into a tank or bowl of water. Have the modeling material, which represents the crew and equipment, on top. If you capsize the boat, it will stay capsized.

3 Add another lump of modeling material underneath the boat, to represent heavy engines or ballast. Add an upturned plastic tub on top to represent a watertight cabin.

4 Now try to capsize it again, and it will flip back upright. This is because the air, trapped underwater by the tub and a heavy weight on top, forces the boat upright again.

How a hydrofoil works

1 Cut a rectangle of plastic, about 2 x 4in, from the lid of the margarine container. Fold it in half. Staple the ends together ½in in from the back edge.

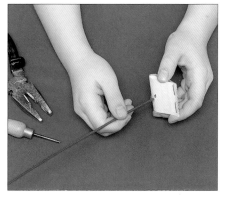

2 Use a bradawl to make a hole in the front of the hydrofoil ½in away from the folded edge. Use pliers to bend ¾in of one end of the wire. Slide the hydrofoil onto the wire.

3 Make sure the hydrofoil moves freely on the wire. Move your hydrofoil in air—it will not lift up, because air is far less dense than water. Pull it through water, and it will rise up the wire.

How a hovercraft works

YOU WILL NEED

How a hydrofoil works:

margarine tub lid, ruler, scissors, stapler, bradawl, pliers, coat hanger wire (ask an adult to cut it), tank or bowl of water.

How a hovercraft works: ruler, styrofoam tray, pencil, balloon, balloon pump, button.

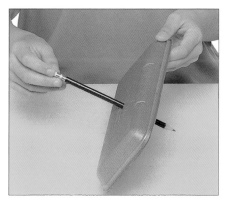

1 Use a ruler to find the middle of the styrofoam tray. Poke a hole through the middle with the pointed end of a pencil. The hole should be about ½in across.

2 Blow up the balloon with the pump, and carefully push its neck through the hole. Keep pinching the neck of the balloon to stop the air from escaping.

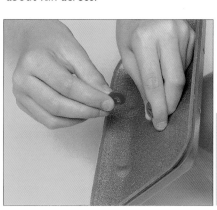

3 Keep pinching the neck of the balloon with one hand, using the other hand to slip the button into the neck. The button will control how fast the air escapes.

4 Place the tray on a table. Air escapes steadily from under the tray's edges, lifting it up a tiny bit. Give the tray a gentle push, and it will skate over the surface.

Submarine action

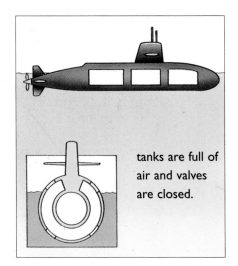

tanks are full of air and valves are closed.

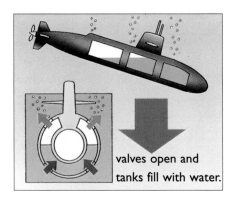

valves open and tanks fill with water.

tanks full— submarine submerged.

air is forced in, so water is forced out

Asubmarine dives by making itself heavier so that it sinks. It surfaces again by making itself lighter. Submarines use large tanks called buoyancy tanks. When the submarine is on the surface, these tanks are full of air. To make the submarine dive, the tanks are flooded with seawater, making the submarine heavy enough to sink. To make the submarine surface again, compressed air is pumped into the tanks, forcing the water out. This makes the submarine lighter, and it floats to the surface. When submarines are underwater, they move up and down using tiny wings called hydroplanes. These work like rudders to control the submarine's direction. Submarines need very strong hulls to prevent them from being crushed by the huge pressure under the water. As submarines dive, the weight of the water pressing down on them becomes greater and greater. You can see how this works by making this model.

YOU WILL NEED

large plastic bottle, sand, plastic funnel, tank of water, two small plastic bottles, bradawl, scissors, ruler, two plastic drinking straws, rubber bands, nonhardening modeling material, two bulldog clips.

Make a submarine

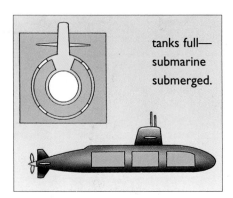

1 Fill the large plastic bottle with sand using a funnel. Fill it until it just sinks in a tank of water. Test the bottle (cap firmly screwed on) to find the right amount of sand.

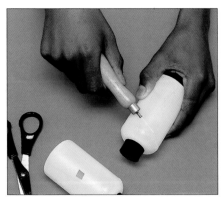

2 Make a large hole (about ½in across) in one side of two small plastic bottles. On the other side make a small hole, big enough for a plastic straw to fit into.

3 Attach the two small bottles to both sides of the large bottle using rubber bands. Twist the small bottles so that the small hole on each one points upward.

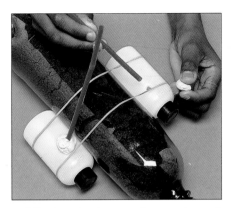

4 Push a plastic straw into each small hole, so that a bit pokes through. Seal around the base of the straws with modeling material to make a watertight joint.

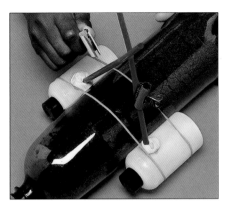

5 Put a small bulldog clip about halfway down each straw. The clips need to be strong enough to squash the straw and stop air from being forced out by the water.

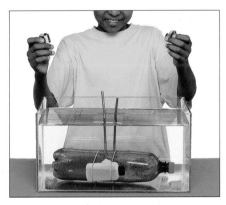

6 Put your model submarine in a tank of water. With the clips on, it should float. Remove the clips and water will flood the buoyancy tanks. The submarine will sink.

7 To make the submarine surface again, blow slowly into both straws at once. The air will force the water out of the buoyancy tanks, and the submarine will rise to the surface.

This is the finished model submarine. You might find that your model sinks bow (front) first, or stern (back) first. If this is the case, level it by shaking the sand evenly inside the bottle.

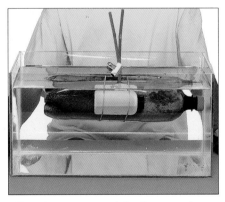

8 When your model submarine has resurfaced, keep blowing slowly into the tanks. Replace each bulldog clip and your model submarine will remain floating on the surface.

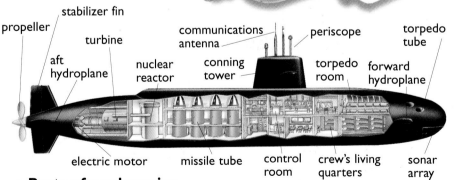

propeller
stabilizer fin
turbine
aft hydroplane
nuclear reactor
communications antenna
conning tower
periscope
torpedo tube
torpedo room
forward hydroplane
electric motor
missile tube
control room
crew's living quarters
sonar array

▲ Parts of a submarine

A modern submarine, such as this nuclear ballistic missile submarine, is almost as long as a football field—100yd. It has an engine and propeller at the stern, and is operated by a crew of 140. Steam drives the turbines that turn the propeller. A submarine's hull is strong, but few submarines can go below 1,600ft.

Making rails

Afull freight or passenger train is heavy, so the track it runs on has to be tough. Nowadays, rails are made from steel, which is a much stronger material than the cast iron used for the first railroads. The shape of the rail also helps to make it strong. If you sliced through a rail from top to bottom, you would see it has an "I"-shaped cross section. The broad, flat bottom narrows into the "waist" of the I, and widens again into a curved head. Most countries use a rail shaped like this.

Tracks are made up of pieces of rail, which are laid on wooden or concrete crossbeams called ties. Train wheels are a set distance apart, so rails must be a set distance apart, too. The distance between rails is called the gauge. This project will show you how to make sets of railroad tracks for the models on the following pages. Make at least two sets of tracks—the more tracks you make, the further your train can travel.

YOU WILL NEED

two sheets of stiff card measuring 10¼ x 4¼in, pencil, ruler, scissors, white glue and glue brush, silver and brown paint, paintbrush, water pot, one sheet of foam board measuring 5 x 8in one sheet of paper measuring 8½ x 11in, masking tape, one sheet of thin card measuring 4 x 2in.

direction of train

guard rails guide wheels and avoid derailment

rodding cables from points signal box

points

points are moved by an electric motor

◀ **Points system**

Trains are switched from one track to another using points. Part of the track (the blade) moves to guide the wheels smoothly from one route to another. A signaller moves the blades by pulling a lever in the signal box. The blade and the lever are connected by metal rods. The lever cannot be pulled unless the signal is clear.

Making tracks

1 Place one 10¼in x 4¼in piece of card lengthways. Draw a line ½in in from each of the outside edges. Draw two more lines, each 2¼in in from the outside edges. This is side A.

2 Turn the card over (side B) and place it lengthways. Measure and draw lines 1½in and 1¾in in from each edge. Repeat steps 1 and 2 with the second piece of 10¼in x 4¼in card.

3 Hold the ruler firmly against one of the lines you have drawn. Use the tip of a pair of scissors to score along the line. Repeat for all lines on both sides of both pieces of card.

4 Place the cards A side up. For each piece in turn, fold firmly along the two lines. Fold up from the scored side. Turn the card over. Repeat for the lines on side B.

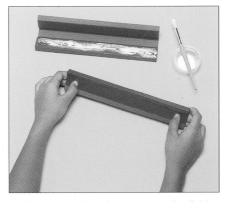

5 With the A side up, press the folds into the I-shape of the rail. Open out again. Glue the B side of the ¾in wide middle section as shown. Repeat for the second rail.

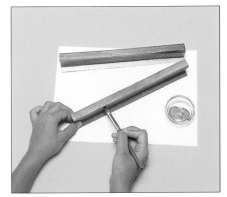

6 Give your two rails a metallic look by painting the upper (A) sides silver. Leave the paint to dry, and then apply a second coat. Leave the second coat to dry.

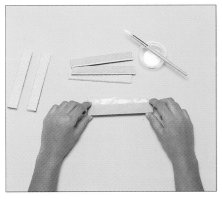

7 Use a pencil and ruler to mark ten 5 x ¾in strips on the foam board. Cut them out. Glue two strips together to make five thick railroad ties. Leave them to dry.

8 Paint the ties brown on their tops and sides, to make them look like wood. Leave them to dry, then apply a second coat of paint. Leave the second coat to dry, too.

9 Lay the ties on the piece of paper, 1¼in apart. Make sure that they are exactly parallel to each other. Run a strip of masking tape down the middle to hold them in place.

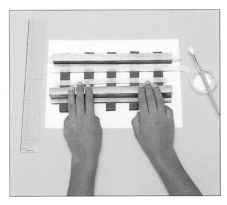

10 Glue the base of a rail, and press into place with the outside edge of the rail ¾in in from the edge of the tie. Repeat with the other track. Secure with masking tape until it is dry.

Make several sets of rails. To join the rails together, roll up the thin card. Insert one end into the top of the I-shape. Push the second rail into the other end.

Rolling stock

The vehicle and machinery that is carried by a modern locomotive's underframe and wheels may weigh up to 100 tons. As bigger and more powerful locomotives were built, more wheels were added to carry the extra weight. Early steam locomotives had only two pairs of wheels. Later steam locomotives had two, three, or four pairs of driving wheels, one pair of which was directly driven from the cylinders. The cylinders house the pistons, whose movement pushes the driving wheels around via a connecting rod.

The other wheels are connected to the driving wheel by a coupling rod, so that they turn at the same time. The small wheels in front of the driving wheels are called leading wheels. The ones behind are the trailing wheels. Locomotives are defined by the total number of wheels they have. For example, a 4-4-0 type locomotive has four leading, four driving, and no trailing wheels. This project shows you how to make an underframe for a 4-4-0 type locomotive, which will run on the tracks described on the previous page. The following page shows how to make a locomotive to sit on the underframe.

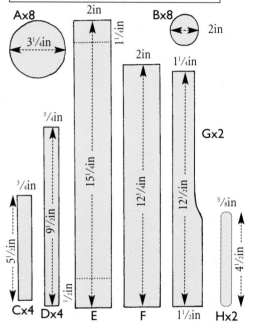

▲ Templates

Draw and cut out the templates from the stiff card. Use a compass to draw the wheel templates A and B.

Make an underframe

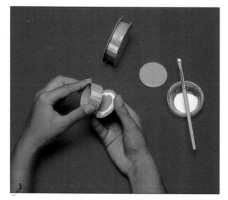

1 Roll the rim templates C and D into rings. Glue and tape to hold. Glue each small wheel circle to each side of a small ring as shown. Repeat for big wheels. Leave to dry.

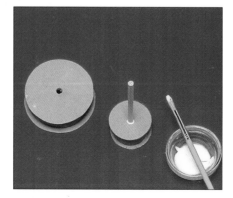

2 Use a pencil to enlarge the compass hole on one side of each wheel. Glue one end of each piece of dowel. Push them into the holes of two big and two small wheels.

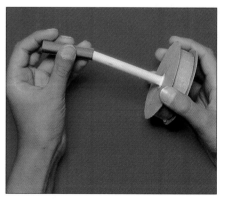

3 Roll the 2 x 2in card into sleeves to fit loosely over each piece of dowel. Tape to hold. Make wheel pairs by fixing the remaining wheels to the dowel as described in step 2.

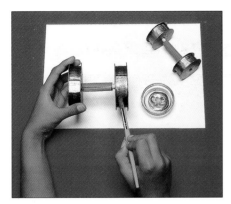

4 When the glue is dry, paint all four pairs of wheels silver. You do not need to paint the dowel axles. Paint two coats, letting the first dry before you apply the second.

5 Use a ruler and pencil to mark eight equal segments on the outside of each wheel. Paint a small circle over the compass hole, and the center of each segment black.

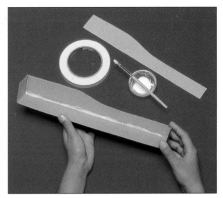

6 Fold along the dotted lines on E. Glue all three straight edges of template G and stick to template E. Repeat this for the other side. Secure all joints with masking tape.

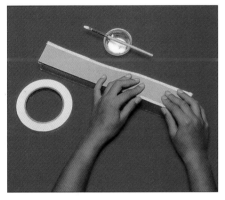

7 Glue the open edges of the underframe. Fit template F on top and hold until firm. Tape over the joints. Give the underframe two coats of black paint. Leave to dry.

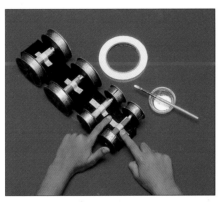

8 Glue the card sleeves to the base of the underframe. Small wheel axles go 1¼in and 2¾in from the front, big wheels 1¼in and 5in from the back. Tape to secure.

9 Paint the coupling rods (H) with a coat of silver paint. Allow the paint to dry thoroughly. Then give the coupling rods a second coat of paint, and leave them to dry.

10 Press a map pin through each end of the coupling rods, about ¼in from the edge. Carefully press the pin into each big wheel about ⅝in beneath the center.

The wheels of the underframe will fit on the model tracks just like those of a real train. In real trains, however, the wheels are mounted in swivelling units called "bogies."

Locomotive

Toy trains started to go on sale during the mid-1800s. Early models were made of brightly painted wood, and often had a wooden track to run along. Soon, metal trains went on sale, many of them made from tinplate (thin sheets of iron or steel coated with tin). Some of these metal toy trains had wind-up, clockwork motors. Clockwork toy trains were first sold in the USA during the 1880s. The most sophisticated model trains were steam-powered, with tiny engines fired by methyl alcohol burners. Later models were powered by electric motors.

Railroad companies often devised special color schemes, called liveries, for their locomotives and carriages. Steam locomotives had brass and copper decoration, and some also carried the company's logo or badge. Many toy trains are also painted in the livery of a real railroad company. The shape of the locomotive you can make in this project has an engine house that is typical of the real locomotives made in the 1930s. The driver and fireman would have shared the cabin of the locomotive. The driver controlled the speed of the train, and the fireman made sure there was a good supply of steam.

YOU WILL NEED

10¼ x 10¼in card, ruler, masking tape, scissors, 4 x 4in card, pencil, white glue and glue brush, stiff card for templates, paints, paintbrush, water pot, underframe from previous project, two thumb tacks, 4¼ x ½in red card, split pin.

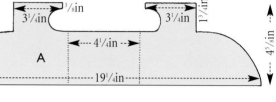

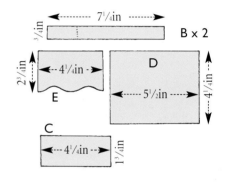

▲ **Templates**
Draw and cut out the templates from the stiff card.

Make a toy train

1 Roll the 10¼ x 10¼in card into an 3¼in diameter tube. Secure it with masking tape. Using the scissors, carefully cut a 2½in slit, 8½in from one end of the tube.

2 Hold the tube upright on the 4 x 4in piece of card. Draw around it. Cut this circle out. Glue the circle to the tube end farthest away from the slit. Tape to secure.

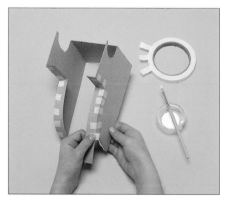

3 Copy and cut out the templates. Fold template A along the dotted lines. Fold templates B upward along the dotted line. Glue both strips to the cabin as shown, and secure with tape.

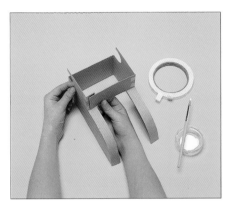

4 When the glue is dry, gently peel off the masking tape. Now glue on template C as shown above. Hold it in place with masking tape until the glue dries, and then remove the tape.

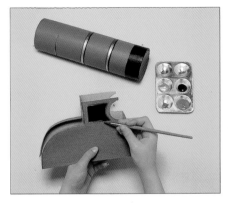

5 Apply two coats of green paint to the outside of the locomotive. Let the first coat dry before applying the second. Then paint the black parts. Add the red and gold last.

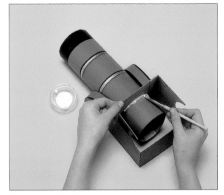

6 Glue around the bottom edge of the cabin front C. Put a little glue over the slit in the tube. Fit the front of the cabin into the slit. Leave the locomotive to one side to dry.

7 Give roof template D two coats of black paint. Let the paint dry between coats. Glue the top edges of the cabin, and place the black roof on top. Leave until dry and firm.

8 Glue the bottom of the cylindrical part of the train to the underframe you made in the "Underframe" project. Press thumb tacks into the back of the cabin and underframe.

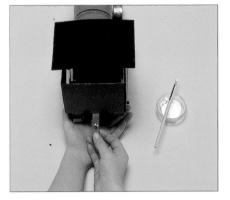

9 Glue both sides of one end of the red strip. Slot this between the underframe and the cabin, between the thumb tacks. When it is firm, fold the strip and insert the split pin.

10 Paint one side of template E black. When it is dry, roll it into a tube and secure with masking tape. Glue the wavy edge and secure it to the front of the locomotive as shown.

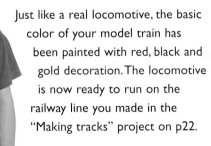

Just like a real locomotive, the basic color of your model train has been painted with red, black and gold decoration. The locomotive is now ready to run on the railway line you made in the "Making tracks" project on p22.

Brake van

Few early steam locomotives had brakes. If the driver needed to stop quickly, he had to throw the engine into reverse. By the early 1860s, braking systems for steam locomotives had been invented. Some passenger carriages also had their own handbrakes that were operated by the carriage guards. A brake van was added to the back of trains, too, but its brakes were operated by a guard riding inside. Old-style brake vans, like the one in this project, sat at the end of the train, so that the guard could make sure that all the carriages stayed coupled.

The problem was that the train driver had no control over the rest of the train. When he wanted to stop, he had to blow the engine whistle to warn each of the carriage guards to apply their brakes. The brakes on a locomotive and its carriages or wagons needed to be linked. This was made possible by the invention of an air-braking system in 1869. When the driver applies the brakes, compressed air travels along pipes that link all the train, and presses brake shoes. Air brakes are now used on nearly all the world's railroads.

YOU WILL NEED

large thick card, small piece of red card for template J, ruler, pencil, scissors, white glue and glue brush, masking tape, four 4in lengths of ¼in-diameter dowel, acrylic paints, paintbrush, water pot, two 1¼in lengths of ¼in-diameter dowel, compass.

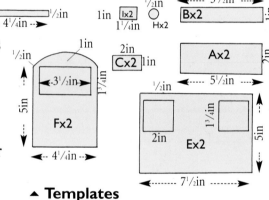

▲ **Templates**

Make a brake van

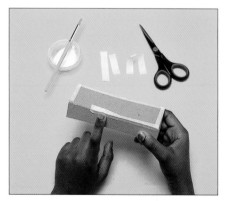

1 Copy the templates onto card and cut them out. Glue templates A, B, and C together to make the underframe as shown. Tape over the joints to secure them.

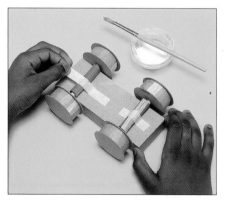

2 Make and paint two pairs of small wheels (2in diameter) following steps 1 through 3 in the "Underframe" project on p24. Glue and tape the wheel pairs to the underframe.

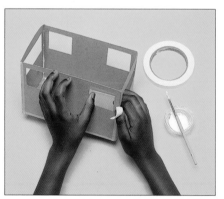

3 Glue the bottom edges of the van sides (E) to the van base (D). Then glue on the van ends (F). Secure the joints with masking tape until the glue is dry.

4 Paint the brake van brown with black details, and the wheels and underframe black and silver. Apply two coats of paint, letting each one dry between coats.

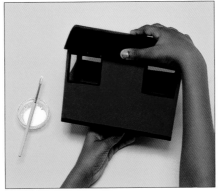

5 Paint one side of template G black. Let the paint dry before applying a second coat. Glue the top edges of the van. Bend the roof to fit on the top of the van as shown.

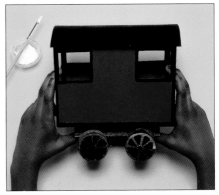

6 Apply glue to the top surface of the underframe. Stick the brake van centrally on top. Press it together until the glue holds firm. Leave the model to dry completely.

7 Roll up templates I into two ¾in tubes to fit loosely over the 1¼in pieces of dowel. Tape to hold. Paint them silver. Paint the buffer templates H black and stick on each dowel.

8 Use a compass to pierce two holes 1in from each side of the van and ⅝in up. Enlarge with a pencil. Glue the end of each dowel buffer. Slot it into the hole. Leave to dry.

9 Cut a ¾in slot between the buffers. Fold the red card template J in half. Glue each open end of the loop, and push them through the slot. Press down to hold firm.

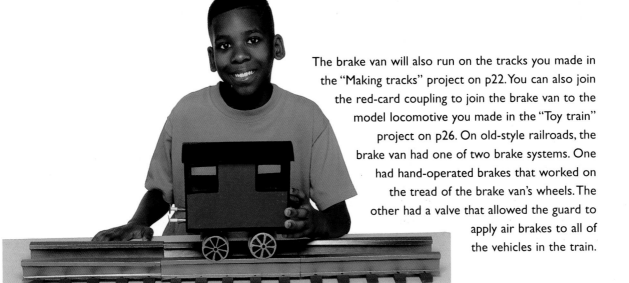

The brake van will also run on the tracks you made in the "Making tracks" project on p22. You can also join the red-card coupling to join the brake van to the model locomotive you made in the "Toy train" project on p26. On old-style railroads, the brake van had one of two brake systems. One had hand-operated brakes that worked on the tread of the brake van's wheels. The other had a valve that allowed the guard to apply air brakes to all of the vehicles in the train.

Making car wheels turn

cylinder head

spark plug

cylinder

piston

con
(connecting) rod

crankshaft

▲ **Working together**

Most car engines have four cylinders arranged like this. You can see the pistons and cylinders. Four rods, one from each piston, turn metal joints attached to the crankshaft. As the rods turn the joints, the crankshaft moves around. This movement is transmitted to the wheels, via the gearbox, which controls how fast the wheels turn relative to the engine.

This experiment shows how one kind of movement—that goes around and around—can be converted into an up-and-down movement. This idea is applied to cars to make the wheels go around, but it happens the other way around. The up-and-down movement of the pistons is changed into the circular motion of the crankshaft and wheels.

When a car engine is switched on, fuel ignites and hot gases are produced in the cylinders. The gases force close-fitting pistons down the cylinders in which they are housed. The pistons are connected to the crankshaft (a rod that connects eventually to the wheels), so that as they move up and down, the crankshaft rotates. This, in turn, makes the wheels go around. One up-and-down movement of a piston results in one turn of the crankshaft. The wheels rotate once for about every three to six turns of the crankshaft.

YOU WILL NEED

shoebox, thin metal rod about $\frac{1}{16}$ in diameter, pliers, jelly jar lid, tape, scissors, thick plastic straw, ruler, pencil, stiff paper, at least four color felt-tipped pens, thin plastic straw.

Changing motion

1 Place the shoebox narrow-side-down on a flat surface. With one hand, push the metal rod through the center, making sure that your other hand will not get jabbed by the rod.

2 Using the pliers, bend the rod at right angles where it comes out of the box. Attach the jelly jar lid to it with tape. Push the lid until it rests against the side of the box.

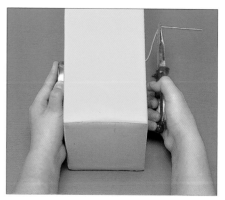

3 Carefully use the pliers to bend the piece of rod sticking out of the other side of the box. This will make a handle for the piston, so that you will be able to turn it easily.

4 Cut a piece of thick plastic straw about 2in long, and tape it to the side of the box close to the jelly jar lid. Make sure that it just sticks up beyond the edge of the box.

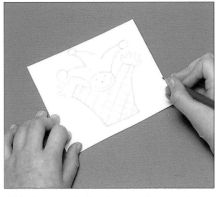

5 Draw a design in pencil on a piece of stiff paper. Copy the jester shown in this project, or draw a simple clown. Choose something that looks good when it moves.

6 Using the felt-tipped pens, color the design until it looks the way you want it to. The more colorful the figure is, the nicer it will look on the top of the piston.

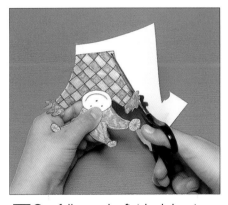

7 Carefully cut the finished drawing out of the paper. Make sure that you have a clean-edged design. Try not to smudge the felt-tipped color with your fingers.

8 Turn the drawing over. Use the tape to attach the thin plastic straw to the bottom of the drawing. About ¾in of straw should be attached.

Place the box on end so the jester is at the top. Turn the handle on the front. As you turn the handle, the jelly jar lid revolves and pushes the jester up and down, like a piston.

9 Slide the straw attached to the drawing into the straw taped to the box. It will come out of the other end. Push down so that the straw touches the edge of the jelly jar lid.

Changing gear

Gears in a car help transfer movement in the most efficient way. They do this by transmitting movement from the crankshaft (which links engine and wheels) to another shaft called the propeller shaft. The propeller shaft rotates more slowly than the crankshaft and adapts the movement, so that the car can cope better with different speeds and efforts, such as starting and going uphill. The change in speed of rotation between the two shafts is controlled from the car's gearbox. As a driver changes gear, toothed wheels that are connected to the crankshaft engage with other toothed wheels joined to the propeller shaft. The difference in the number of teeth on each wheel determines the number of times the wheels turn, as the first project demonstrates. The second experiment shows how gear wheels work in a car. The larger corrugated card wheel has more teeth than the two smaller wheels.

crankshaft

propeller shaft

high gear

low gear

▲ **Wheels within wheels**
The car's engine turns the crankshaft with different-sized gears (toothed wheels) on it. High gears are used for more speed, because the big wheel turns the small wheel faster. The gear system is called the transmission—it transmits (moves) the engine's power to the car's wheels. Most cars have five gears. The biggest is needed for slow speeds, and the smallest for high speeds.

YOU WILL NEED

compass, ruler, pencil, 8½ x 11in sheet of white paper, black pen, scissors, 8½ x 11in sheet of thin card, two strips of corrugated card, tape, three colored felt-tipped pens.

Drawing the gears

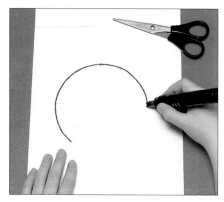

1 Using the compass, trace a 5½in-diameter circle on the paper. Draw over it with the pen and cut it out. On the card, trace, draw, and cut out an 4¼in-diameter circle.

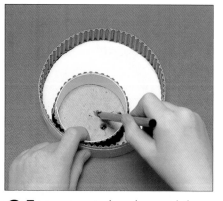

2 Tape corrugated card around the circles. Make a hole in the small circle wide enough for the tip of a felt-tipped pen. Turn the small wheel inside the larger. Trace the path in felt-tipped pen.

3 Make a second hole in the small wheel. Turn the small gear inside the larger using another felt-tipped pen. Make a third hole in the small wheel and use a third color pen.

Three-gear machine

1 Use the compass to trace one 5½in-diameter and two 4¼in-diameter circles on the card. Draw around the circle edges with the pen, and cut the circles out.

2 Carefully wrap the strips of corrugated card around the circles, using one strip per circle, corrugated side out. Tape each strip to the bottom of the circles.

As you turn the gears, notice how they move in opposite directions to each other. Now you have a three-gear machine, where the energy from each gear is being transferred to the others, just like the gears in a car.

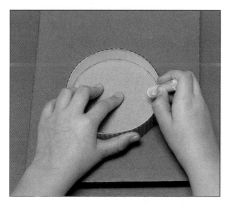

3 Place the largest gear wheel on the piece of fiberboard. Hold the gear down and glue the dowel on to the side of the gear base at the edge of the wheel. Leave it until it is dry.

4 Position all three gears on the fiberboard, with the edges just touching each other. Pin each of them firmly to the fiberboard with a map pin, but allow them to turn.

5 Gently turn the dowel on the largest gear. As that gear turns, the two others that are linked together by the corrugated card will turn against it.

Car control

Cars have two kinds of brakes. Parking brakes lock the rear wheels when the car is standing still. Disk brakes slow down the car when it is moving, in the same way that the sandpaper slows the model wheel in the first experiment.

The second project shows how a device called the camshaft controls the flow of fuel into the cylinders. The camshaft is designed so as to have a regular action that opens one valve and closes another at the same time. Inlet valves let fuel and air into the engine, and burned waste gases are removed via the outlet valves. The camshaft controls make the engine run smoothly.

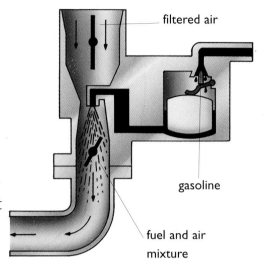

▲ The carburetor

Fuel and air enter the carburetor in just the right quantities for the car to run smoothly. The mixture is then fed into the cylinders. Pressing the accelerator pedal in a car allows more air and fuel into the engine to make it run faster, so speeding up the car.

YOU WILL NEED

Disk brakes: scissors, 16in piece of fabric, circular card box with lid, tape, pencil, 8in piece of ⅝in-diameter wood dowel, white glue, glue brush, 2¾ x 4¼in medium sandpaper, 2½ x 4in wooden block, two plastic cups, insulation tape.

How valves work: scissors, 4½in square of stiff card, masking tape, cardboard tube with plastic lid, pencil.

Stopping ▶

When a driver presses the brake pedal, a piston presses together two pads, one on either side of the disk to which the wheel is attached. This strong grip stops the disk from turning, and as the disk slows, so do the wheels.

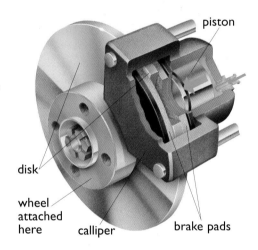

piston

disk

wheel attached here

calliper

brake pads

Disk brakes

1 Use the scissors to cut a narrow 16in strip from the fabric. You may have to use special fabric cutting scissors if your ordinary scissors are not sharp enough.

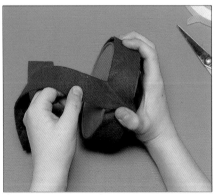

2 Take the strip of fabric you have cut out, and wrap it around the rim of the circular cardboard box. Secure it firmly in place with small pieces of tape.

3 Make a hole in the center of the box's lid with a pencil. Twist the pencil until it comes through the base of the box. Now gently push the wood dowel through both holes.

4 Spread lots of glue onto the sandpaper's smooth side. Wrap the sandpaper carefully over the top of the wood block. Pressing firmly, stick it together. Leave it to dry.

5 Stand two plastic cups upside down. Rest either end of the dowel on each cup. Cut two small pieces of insulation tape. Use them to fix each end of the dowel to the cup bases.

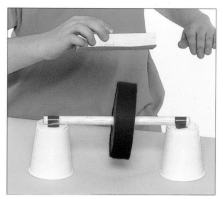

6 Spin the lid fast on the dowel. As it spins, bring the sandpaper into contact with the edge of the lid. Test your brake disk to see how quickly you can stop the lid.

How valves work

1 Use scissors to cut a ½ x 4½in strip from the stiff card. Double it over in the center. Hold it with your fingertips. Bend the two ends of the card away from one another.

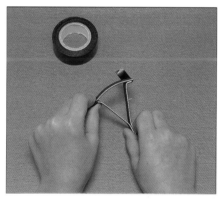

2 Cut a ½ x 1½in strip from the original piece of card. Use masking tape to fix the card strip to the bent bottom ends of the first piece. This makes a triangle shape.

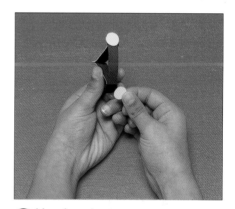

3 Use the scissors to cut out two small circle shapes from the original piece of card. Use masking tape to secure them to the bottom piece of the triangle you have made.

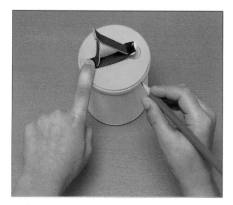

4 Put the stiff card triangle on top of the cardboard tube. The circles should touch the plastic lid. With a pencil, mark the position where the circles sit on the lid.

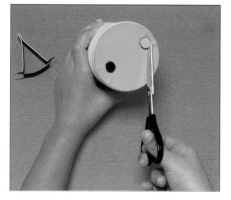

5 Using the scissors, carefully cut around the pencil marks you have made in the plastic lid of the tube. These form an inlet and an outlet. As one valve opens, the other will close.

6 Now you can rock the triangle back and forth, to cover and uncover the two holes. This is just how a camshaft opens and shuts the inlet and outlet valves in a car's cylinder.

Keeping cool

The explosion of fuel and air that fires a car's engine generates a great deal of heat. Friction (rubbing together of two surfaces), as the engine parts move together at speed, also creates heat. If the heat level is not kept down, the engine stops working. Metal parts expand, seize up, and stop. To cool the engine, water from the car's radiator is pumped around the hottest parts of the engine—the combustion chambers, where the fuel ignites, and the cylinders.

▲ Mass production

All the separate parts of a car are mass-produced and then assembled (put together) on a production line to make the finished vehicle. Almost all cars are assembled on production lines today. Robots do much of the work.

The moving water carries heat away from the hottest parts of the engine. The radiator cools the hot water from the engine by using a fan. The fan is driven by a belt connected to the engine. This project shows how a belt transfers turning movement from one shaft to another. This is how a car's engine turns the fan belt.

YOU WILL NEED

---

ruler, 6¼in square of thin cloth, scissors, five reels of thread, glue stick, 8½ x 11in wooden board, pencil, five flat-headed nails 1½in long, hammer, 1yd x 1in velvet ribbon, tape, compass, five pieces of 4in-square colored card, five wooden skewers.

Fan belt

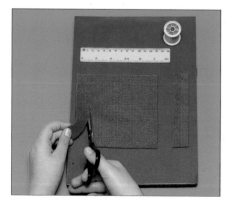

1 Using the ruler, measure five 1in-wide strips on the thin cloth. The height of the reels of thread should be more than 1in. Use the scissors to cut out each strip.

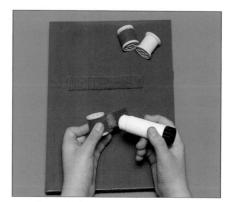

2 Wrap one of the fabric strips around each of the five reels of thread. Glue each strip at the end, so that it sits firmly around the reel and will not come loose.

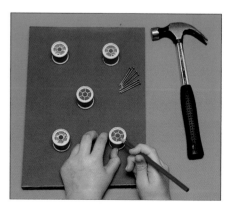

3 Place the reels on the wooden board as shown above. Trace the outlines with a pencil. Put the nails through the center of the reels, and carefully hammer them into the board.

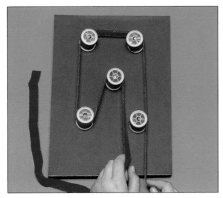

4 Wind the ribbon around the reels, with the velvet side against four of the reels. Cut the ribbon at the point where you can join both ends around the fifth reel.

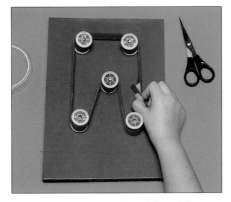

5 Tape the two ends of the ribbon together firmly. Make sure that the ribbon wraps firmly around all of the five reels, but not so tightly that it can't move.

6 Use the compass to draw circles about ¾in in diameter onto the five pieces of colored card. Then carefully draw freehand spiral shapes inside each circle.

7 Use the scissors to cut each spiral out of each of the pieces of colored card. Start from the outside edge, and gradually work your way in along the lines of the spiral.

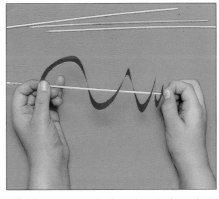

8 Tape one end of each spiral to the end of a skewer. Wind the other end of the spiral around the skewer stick a few times. Tape it close to the opposite end of the skewer.

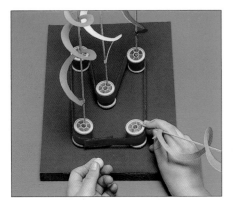

9 Put a small amount of tape onto the end of each wooden skewer. Then place each skewer into one of the empty holes in the top of each reel of thread.

Now you are ready to turn the belt. Like a fan belt in a car, it turns the fans around. This is a five-fan machine. You can add more fans if you like.

Prototype car

When you make your model car, choose the colors carefully. Do you want bright colors that will be noticed easily, or cool, fashionable colors? Car manufacturers call in teams of people to help them decide what a car should look like. Stylists, and design and production engineers join forces with the sales team to develop cars they hope people will buy. They think about the colors, how much people are prepared to pay, and what features they want, from air-conditioning to special car seats.

Before a new car is launched to the public, detailed models are made and tested to investigate the car's aerodynamics (how air flows over its shape). Finally, a prototype (early version) of the car is built and tested for road handling, engine quality, and comfort.

Wire basket ▶

Car designers today make use of CAD (computer-aided design) software to help them create a three-dimensional image of a new car design. Wire-frame (see-through) computer images show the car from any angle. They also show how all the parts of the car fit together.

Model car

1 Draw and cut out four 1in and eight 2½in diameter card circles. Glue the 2½in circles together to make four wheels. Glue a 1in circle to the center of each wheel.

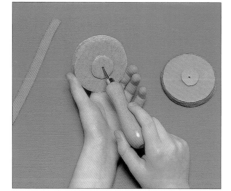

2 Use the bradawl to make a hole in the center of each wheel. Cut four ⅛in strips of colored card. Wrap one each around the wheel rims. Glue the overlapping ends.

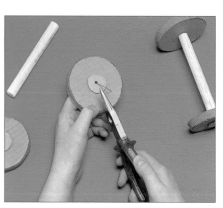

3 Push straightened paper clips into the holes, and bend the outer ends with pliers. Fix the wheels to the two pieces of dowel by pushing the paper clips into the ends.

4 Cut a piece of card to 2¾ x 6in. Trim one end to make it 2½in wide. Tape the two axles to the card, one at each end. Make sure they are long enough for the wheels to rotate freely.

5 Cut a piece of card 3¼ x 14in. Double it over and bend it into a British cab shape. Tape the two loose ends together. Stick the base of the cab shape to the car base.

6 Cut two cardboard shapes 6in long and 4in high. Trim them with the scissors to the same shape as the side of your car cab. Attach the sides to the cab with tape.

Decorate your car

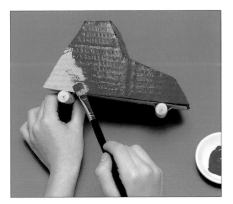

1 Remove the wheels from your car. Paint the sides and top of the cab with one of the two colors of paint. Leave it to dry. Then paint it with the same color again, and leave it to dry.

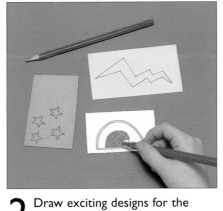

2 Draw exciting designs for the sides of the car and a driver to go behind the windscreen. Draw some head lamps and some exhaust fumes. Add color with the felt-tipped pens.

Replace the wheels when they are dry. Now your car looks just like a real vehicle. Cut photographs of cars from magazines for more design ideas.

3 Let the paint dry for a couple of hours. Cut the designs out of the card. Glue them to the sides and back of the car. Paint the wheels with the color of paint you haven't used.

Parachutes and balloons

Parachutes fall slowly because air is trapped beneath them. They are deliberately designed to have very high drag. Drag is the force that works against the direction of anything that flies through the air. The amount of drag depends on the shape. A fat, lumpy shape, like the parachute in the first project, has lots of drag and falls slowly.

Hot air balloons rise into the air, because the hot air inside them is lighter than the air outside. Real balloons use gas burners, but the project here uses a hair dryer to heat the air in the balloon.

YOU WILL NEED

felt-tipped pen, a large plate, thin fabric, scissors, needle, thread, tape, plastic thread reel.

Mini-parachute jump

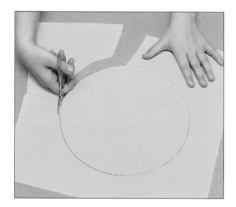

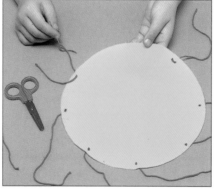

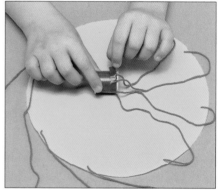

1 Use the felt-tipped pen to draw around the plate on the fabric. Using the scissors, carefully cut out the circle to make what will be the parachute's canopy.

2 Make about eight equally spaced marks around the edge of the circle. Use a needle to sew on one 12in long piece of thread to each point you have marked.

3 Use tape to secure the free end of each thread to a reel. Use a plastic reel, because a wooden one will be too heavy for your parachute.

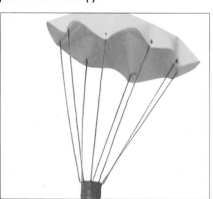

4 Hold the parachute so that the canopy is open and the thread reel dangles down. Stand by an upstairs window, or use a step-ladder to get as high as you can—but be very careful!

Let your parachute go from as high up as possible. As it falls, the canopy will open and fill with air. The larger the canopy, the slower the parachute will fall.

Ballooning around

YOU WILL NEED

pencil, card, ruler, scissors,

sheets of tissue paper,

glue stick, hair dryer.

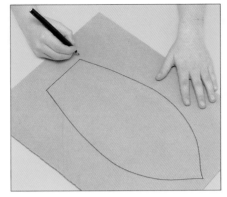

1 To make a template, draw a petal shape on card and carefully cut it out. The shape should be 12in long and 4½in across with a flat bottom edge.

2 Draw around your template on seven pieces of colored tissue paper. Be very careful not to rip the tissue paper with the tip of your pencil.

3 Use the pair of scissors to carefully cut out the shapes you have drawn. You should now have seven petals that are all the same size and shape.

To fly your balloon, hold its neck open and fill the inside with hot air from a hair dryer. After ten seconds, switch off the hair dryer and let go of your balloon to launch it into the air.

4 Glue along one edge of a petal. Lay another petal on top, and press it down. Open it out and stick on another petal in the same way. Keep going until the balloon is complete.

Streamlined design

Think of a sleek canoe moving through the water. Its streamlined shape hardly makes any ripples as it passes. Streamlined shapes also move easily through the air. They have low drag (air resistance). Angular shapes have more drag than rounded ones. The shape of a fast-moving fish has to be very streamlined. A fish such as a tuna has a blunt front end, is broadest about a third of the way along, then tapers towards the tail. This creates less drag as it moves through water than a shape with a pointed front end that broadens at the back. Water flows along each side of the tuna to rejoin without creating turbulence. The "Shape race" gives you a chance to design and test your own streamlined shapes.

Just as things that are moving in the air experience drag, so do stationary objects in the wind. Kites, such as the one here, are held up in the air by drag from the wind. For more than 3,000 years, people have been making and flying kites. The essential, but simple, secret is that it must be as light as possible for its size, so that it catches as much wind as possible. The kite design shown in this project has been used for many hundreds of years. Try flying it first of all in a steady wind, and experiment with the position of the bridle and the length of the tail.

YOU WILL NEED

pen, ruler, two bamboo canes (one about two-thirds as long as the other), string, scissors, tape, sheet of thin fabric or plastic, fabric glue, colored paper.

▲ How air flows work

Air flows in gentle curves around the streamlined shape (*top*). Angles and sharp curves break up the flow and increase drag (*bottom*).

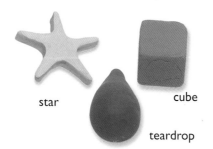

star
cube
teardrop

▲ Shape race

Make different shapes (as shown above) from balls of modeling material that are exactly the same size. Race your shapes in water—the most streamlined shape should reach the bottom first.

Make a kite

1 To make the frame, mark the center of the short cane and mark one-third of the way up the long cane. Tie the canes together crosswise at the marks with string.

2 Tape string around the ends of the canes and secure it at the top. This will stop the canes from moving, and it will also support the edges of your finished kite.

3 Lay the frame on top of the sheet of fabric or plastic. Cut around it, ¾in away from the kite's edge. This will give you enough to fold over the string outline.

4 Fold each edge of the material over the frame, and stick the edges down firmly with fabric glue (or tape if you are making the kite from plastic). Let the glue dry.

5 Tie a piece of string to the long cane, as shown—this is called the bridle. Tie the end of the ball of string to the middle of the bridle to make the tether.

6 Fold sheets of paper in zigzags. Tie them at about 10in intervals along a piece of string that is about twice as long as the kite. Glue or tie the tail to the bottom tip of the kite.

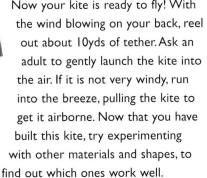

bridle

tail

tassel

tether

Now your kite is ready to fly! With the wind blowing on your back, reel out about 10yds of tether. Ask an adult to gently launch the kite into the air. If it is not very windy, run into the breeze, pulling the kite to get it airborne. Now that you have built this kite, try experimenting with other materials and shapes, to find out which ones work well.

Curve and lift

Birds, gliders, and airplanes all have wings. Their wings can be all sorts of different shapes and sizes, but they all have the same airfoil design. This means that the top side of the wing is more curved than the underside. The airfoil shape provides lift when air moves over it. Air flows faster over the curved upper surface than over the flatter lower surface. This reduces the air pressure above the wing, and lets the higher air pressure underneath lift it up.

You can make and test a model airfoil by following the instructions in these projects. In the frisbee project, the shape of the frisbee allows the air to move smoothly over and under it. The frisbee spins as it flies. The spinning motion helps to steady it. The second project shows you how moving air, in this case, from an electric fan or hair dryer, can lift the wings with an airfoil shape upward.

Fly a frisbee

1 Place the plate face down on the card, and draw around it with a pencil. Cut out the circle of card. Draw slots ¾ in deep around the edge and cut these, as shown.

2 The cut slots around the edge will make tabs. Bend the tabs down slightly. Overlap them a little and stick them together with small pieces of tape.

Fly your frisbee outside, away from people. Hold it at the front and spin it away from you and up. It should glide through the air smoothly as the air pressure above it is reduced. Play toss-and-catch games with your friends. You could even have your own championship match! Commercial frisbees were introduced into the USA in the 1950s.

Airfoil antics

I Use a ruler to measure a rectangle of colored paper about 6in wide and 8in long. Use scissors to carefully cut out the shape. This will be your wing.

2 Fold the paper over, approximately in half. Use tape to fix the top edge ½in away from the bottom edge. Take care not to crease the paper as you do this.

3 Cut out and stick on a small paper fin near the rear edge of your wing, as shown. This will keep the wing facing into the airflow when you test it.

4 With a sharp pencil, carefully poke a hole through the top and bottom of your wing, near the front edge. Push a straw through the holes and glue it in place in the middle.

Hold the thread tight, and ask a friend to blow air from a fan or hair dryer over the wing. Watch it take off! This happens because the shape decreases the air pressure above the wing.

5 Cut a 1yd-long piece of thick thread and thread it through the straw. Make sure that the thread can slide easily through the straw and does not catch.

Jet propulsion

A jet engine produces thrust from a roaring jet of super-hot gas. Its construction looks complicated, but the way it works is very simple. A powerful jet of gas moving in one direction produces thrust in the other direction. Imagine you are standing on a skateboard and squirting a powerful hose forward. Jet propulsion will push you backward. This reaction has been known for nearly 2,000 years, but it was not until the 1930s that it was applied to an engine.

In the first experiment, you can make a jet zoom along a string. The jet engine is like a balloon that produces thrust from escaping air. The second project demonstrates how a turbine works. Hot air produced by the gas jet turns the blades of the turbine. The turbine drives the fan at the front of the jet engine. These projects may seem simple, but they use the same scientific principles that propel all jet airplanes through the air.

YOU WILL NEED

Balloon jet: long, thin balloon, scissors, tape, drinking straw, string.
Turbine lights: aluminum pie tin, scissors, compass, protractor, ruler, pin, 3in length of ⅛in dowel, tape, bead, thread reel, nonhardening modeling material, plate, four night light candles, matches.

Balloon jet

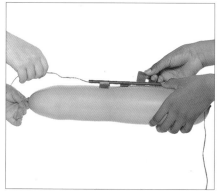

I Blow up the balloon and, while a friend holds the neck, tape the straw to its top. Thread the string through the straw and, holding it level, tie it to something to keep it in place.

▲ **Practical plane**
This passenger plane has four engines, two on each wing. Jet engines have revolutionized international travel. Passenger planes carry millions of travelers around the world every year.

2 Let go of the neck of the balloon. A stream of air jets backward and produces thrust. This propels the balloon forward along the string at high speed.

Turbine lights

1 Using scissors, cut out the bottom of a large aluminum pie tin as evenly as possible. Make a small hole in the center with the point of the compass.

2 Mark a smaller circle in the center. Use a protractor to mark 16 equal sections of 22.5 degrees, and cut along each one to the inner circle. Use one scissor cut along each line, if possible.

3 Angle the blades by holding the inner tip and twisting the outer edges 20 to 30 degrees. The center of the inner tip should be flat, in line with the center of the disk.

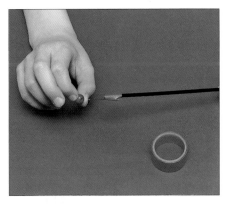

4 Tape the blunt end of the pin to one end of the dowel. Finish it off neatly and trim if necessary. Place the bead on the pin. This will allow the finished turbine to spin freely.

◀ Jet engine

The huge blades at the front of a jet engine suck in air and compress it. Fuel burns in the air to produce jets of hot air that blast from the rear of the engine, producing thrust.

5 Put the dowel in the reel and press the reel into the modeling material in the centre of the plate. Place the four candles on the plate around the reel.

Place the hole in the center of the turbine over the pin. Ask an adult to light the candles. Hot air will spin the blades.

Propeller flight

Propellers work in two different ways. When a propeller spins, it makes air move past it. Propeller-driven aircraft use this effect to produce thrust. Moving air also causes the propeller to spin. The projects here look at propellers working in these two ways. In the first one, you can make a simple paper propeller called a spinner. As the spinner falls, moving air rushes past the blades, making it revolve. This acts just like the fruits and seeds of maple and sycamore trees, which have twin propeller blades. As they drop from the tree, they spin and catch the wind, and are carried far away.

In the second project, you can make a spinning propeller fly upward through the air. The propellerlike blades are set at an angle, like the blades of a fan. They whirl around and make air move. The moving air produces thrust and lifts the propeller upward.

Children first flew propellers like these 600 years ago in China.

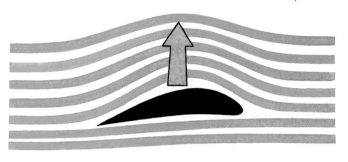

▲ Lift off

An airfoil's curved shape causes the air to flow faster over its upper surface than its lower surface. This reduces pressure from above and causes lift.

In a spin

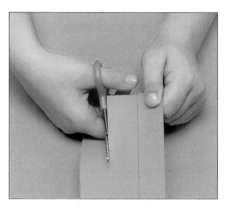

1 Take a piece of paper, 6 x 3½in, and draw a T-shape on it, as shown in the picture above. With a pair of scissors, cut along the two long lines of the T.

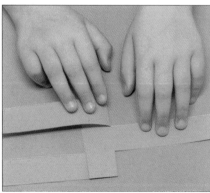

2 Fold one side strip forwards and one backwards, as shown above, making two blades and a stalk. Attach a paper clip to the bottom. Open the blades flat.

3 Drop the spinner and watch what happens. Before dropping it again, try giving each blade a twist to make your spinner spin around even faster.

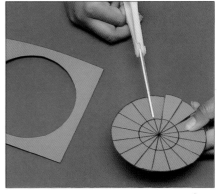

Let's twist

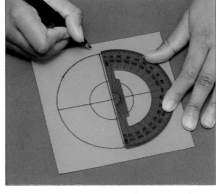

1 With the compass, draw a circle 4in across on the card. Draw a circle 1½in across in the centre. With the protractor, draw lines across the circle, dividing it into 16 equal sections.

2 Carefully cut out the circle and along the lines to the smaller circle. Twist the blades sideways a little. Try to give each blade the same amount of twist, about 20 or 30 degrees.

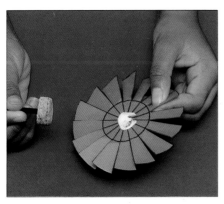

3 Make a hole in the center of the cork slice with a bradawl. Put glue on the end of the dowel, and push it into the hole. Glue the cork to the middle of the propeller.

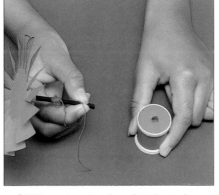

4 When the glue has dried, wind a long piece of string around the dowel. Drop the dowel into the thread reel launcher. You are now ready for a test flight.

Pull steadily on the string to move the propeller around. As the end of the string comes off, the blades produce enough thrust to lift the spinning propeller out of the launcher and into the air.

Model planes

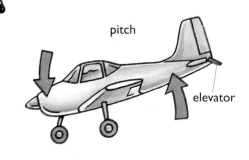

ailerons

roll

Although a model is much smaller than a real full-size aircraft, it flies in exactly the same way. The control surfaces on the wings and the tail of a model plane or real aircraft work by changing the way in which air flows over the aircraft. This allows the pilot to steer the aircraft in different directions. Working together, the rudder and movable flaps called ailerons on the rear edge of each wing make the plane turn to the left or right. Moving flaps called elevators on the tail make the nose of the plane go up or down.

pitch

elevator

The scientific rules of flying are the same for any aircraft, from an airliner weighing 350 tons to this model made from paper, tape, and a drinking straw. Making this model plane allows you to see how control surfaces, such as the aileron, rudder, and elevators, work. The flight of any plane is very sensitive to the angle of the controls. They need to be only a slight angle from their flat position to make the plane turn. Too big an angle will make the model unstable.

rudder

yaw

▲ How to fly a plane
To turn the aircraft (yaw), the pilot turns the rudder to one side. To make the aircraft descend or climb (pitch), the pilot adjusts the elevators on the tailplane. To roll (tilt or bank) the aircraft to the left or right, the ailerons are raised on one wing and lowered on the other.

Glide along

YOU WILL NEED
pencil, set square, ruler, paper, scissors, glue stick, tape, drinking straw, paper clips or nonhardening modeling material.

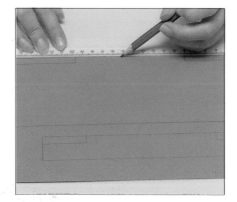

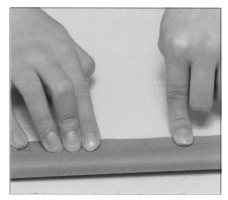

1 Draw two paper rectangles, 8¾ x 4in and 8 x 1¼in. Mark ailerons 2½ x ½in on two corners of the larger one. Mark two elevators 1½ x ½in on the other. Cut them out.

2 To make the wings, wrap the larger rectangle over a pencil, and glue along the edges. Remove the pencil and make cuts along the ½in lines to allow the ailerons to move.

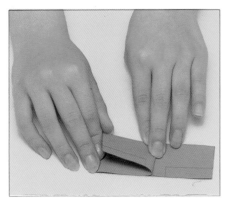

3 To make the tail, fold the smaller rectangle in half twice to form a W. Glue its center to make the fin. Cut along the two ½in lines. Make a ½in cut on the fin to make a rudder.

4 Use tape to fix the wings and tail to the drinking straw (the plane's fuselage, or body). Position the wings about one quarter of the way along the straw.

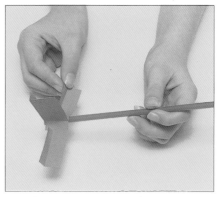

5 Try adjusting the control surfaces. Bend the elevators on the tail slightly up. This will make the plane climb as it flies. Bend the elevators down to make it dive.

6 Bend the left-hand aileron up and the right-hand aileron down the same amount. Bend the rudder to the left. This will make the plane turn to the left as it flies.

Launch your plane by throwing it steadily straight ahead. To make it fly even farther, use paper clips or modeling material to weight the nose.

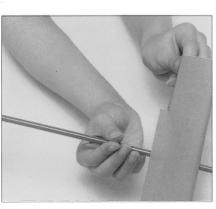

7 Bend the right-hand aileron up and the left-hand aileron down. Bend the rudder slightly to the right and the plane will turn to the right. Can you make it fly in a circle?

Escaping from Earth

The function of a space rocket is to carry a satellite or astronauts into Space. To do this, it has to overcome gravity (the force that pulls everything down to Earth). If a rocket's engines are not powerful enough, gravity will win and pull the rocket back to Earth. With more powerful engines, the rocket's attempt to fly into Space is exactly equalled by the pull of gravity. With these two forces in perfect balance, a spacecraft will continue to circle the Earth. If the rocket is even more powerful, it can fly fast enough to escape from Earth's gravity altogether and head toward the Moon and the planets. The speed that it needs to reach to do this is called escape velocity. You can see this in action by trying an experiment using a magnet and ball-bearings. You can also try launching your own cork model rocket from a plastic bottle.

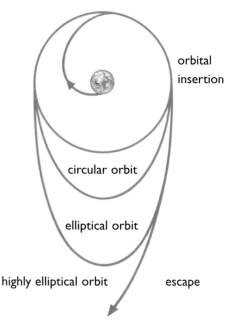

orbital
insertion

circular orbit

elliptical orbit

highly elliptical orbit   escape

▲ Escape velocity

To go into orbit around the Earth, a spacecraft must reach a velocity of at least 17,500mph. Depending on how fast it is travelling, the spacecraft may go into a circular, elliptical, or highly elliptical orbit. If it reaches a velocity of 25,000mph, the spacecraft escapes from the Earth's gravity altogether.

Launch a rocket

1 Place a teaspoon of baking soda directly in the middle of a 4 x 8in piece of paper towel. Roll up the towel, and twist the ends to keep the baking soda fuel inside.

2 Pour half a cup of water and the same amount of vinegar into the bottle. Fix paper streamers or a ribbon to the the cork with a pin. Drop the paper towel inside the bottle.

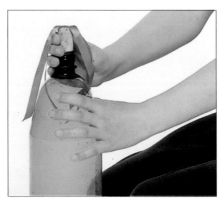

3 Push the cork in immediately so that it is a snug fit, but not too tight. Quickly take the bottle outside. Then move at least 3yd away from it and watch what happens.

A chemical reaction between the vinegar (representing liquid oxygen) and baking soda (representing fuel) produces carbon dioxide gas. The gas pressure inside the bottle pushes against the cork. The cork is blasted into the air like a rocket lifting off. However, in a real rocket, the gas is jetted out of the actual spacecraft, propelling it forward.

YOU WILL NEED

Launch a rocket: baking soda, paper towel, water, vinegar, ½ gallon plastic bottle, paper streamers or ribbon, cork, pin.

Escaping from gravity: thin card, ruler, pencil, scissors, magnetic strip, white glue, glue brush, 4 x 2in piece of plastic, baking tray, nonhardening modeling material, tape, ball-bearings.

Escaping from gravity

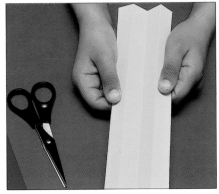

1 Measure out a 12 x 4in strip of thin card using a ruler. Cut it out with the scissors. Fold it lengthwise into four sections to form an M-shaped trough.

2 Cut the magnetic strip into five short pieces. Glue these short strips to the plastic base, so that they form a large, square bar magnet, as shown above.

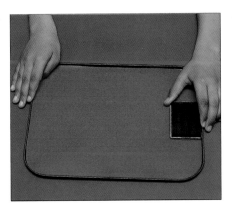

3 Fix the magnet firmly to one end of the tray with some of the modeling material. Position it roughly in the middle. The magnet simulates the pull of the Earth's gravity.

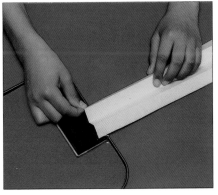

4 Position one end of the trough over the edge of the magnet. Attach it to the magnet with tape. The trough represents the path of a rocket as it ascends into orbit.

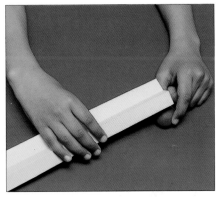

5 Roll the remaining modeling material into a round ball. Position the ball underneath the other end of the M-shaped trough. This raises the trough at a slight angle.

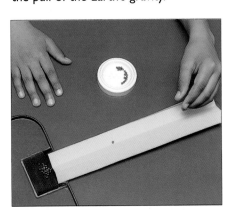

6 At the end of the trough, place a ball-bearing and let it roll down. It sticks to the magnet. The ball-bearing's velocity along the trough isn't fast enough to escape the magnet's pull.

Raise the trough and roll another ball-bearing along it. The steeper angle increases the ball-bearing's velocity. Keep raising the trough and rolling ball-bearings, until one shoots past the magnet. It has then achieved escape velocity!

Rocket launch

Space rockets rely on jet propulsion to fly. When the rocket burns its fuel, a stream of hot gases roars out from the tail end and the rocket surges forward. Jets flying lower than 82,000ft can burn their fuel using oxygen from the air. Space rockets need to carry oxygen with them, because above 82,000ft, the air thins out and there is not enough oxygen.

Deep in the sea, octopuses also rely on jet propulsion to escape from their enemies. They squirt out a jet of water and shoot off in the opposite direction.

This experiment shows you how to make and fly a rocket that uses jet propulsion. The thrust of a rocket depends on the mass of propellant that it shoots out every second. Water is a much better propellant than hot gas, because it is so much heavier.

Follow these instructions carefully and your rocket could fly about 80ft above the ground. You may need adult to help make some parts of this rocket and to launch it. When you are ready for a test flight, set your rocket up in an open space, well away from trees and buildings. This rocket is very powerful—you must not stand over it while it is being launched. Wear clothes that you do not mind getting very wet!

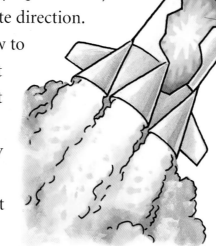

oxygen

hydrogen

combustion chamber

▲ Inside a rocket

This is a liquid-fueled rocket. It carries liquid oxygen to burn its fuel (liquid hydrogen). The hydrogen and oxygen are pumped into the combustion chamber. The hydrogen burns furiously in the oxygen. The exhaust produces immense thrust.

Make a rocket

YOU WILL NEED
white card, pen, ruler, colored card, scissors, plastic bottle, strong tape, funnel, pitcher of water, cork, bradawl, air valve, plastic tube, bicycle pump.

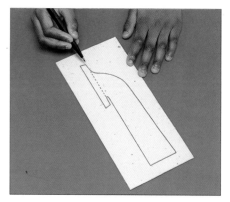

Rockets have fins to make them fly straight. Draw out this fin template (it is about 8in long) on plain card and use it to cut out four fins from colored card.

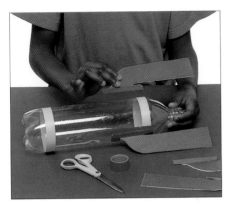

2 Decorate your bottle to look like a rocket. Fold the tab at the top of each fin. Use long pieces of strong tape to attach the fins to the bottle firmly.

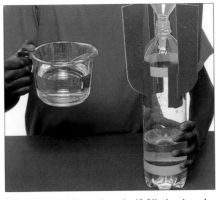

3 Use the funnel to half-fill the bottle with water. (The water is the propellant. Compressed air above the water will provide the energy that makes the thrust.)

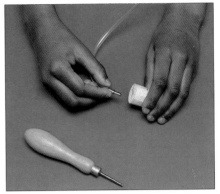

4 Use the bradawl to drill a hole carefully through the cork. Push the wide end of the air valve into the plastic tube. Push the valve through the hole in the cork.

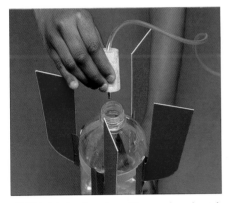

5 Hold the bottle with one hand, and push the cork and the valve into the neck of the bottle using the other hand. Push it in firmly so that the cork does not slide out too easily.

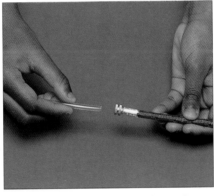

6 Attach the other end of the plastic tube to the bicycle pump. Turn your rocket the right way up—you are now ready to launch your rocket outside.

Look for a launch site far away from trees and buildings. Stand the rocket on its tail fins, and tell everyone to stand well back. Start pumping. Bubbles of air will rise up through the water. When the pressure in the bottle gets high enough, the cork and the water will be forced out and the rocket will fly upward. Be careful not to stand over the bottle!

Going to the Moon

Plotting a course through Space is more complicated than traveling over land. Pilots follow natural features, such as hills, valleys, and rivers; at high altitudes, they use radio beacons on the ground or satellite signals. The problem with traveling from the Earth to the Moon is that both are moving, as the first project illustrates. The second project shows how a heavy craft gets to the Moon. Staged rockets release their sections as they progress into Space, so reducing the weight of the rocket.

If a spacecraft was aimed straight at the Moon when it set off from Earth, the Moon would have moved on around its orbit by the time the craft arrived. If the spacecraft corrected its direction to follow the Moon's orbit, it would use too much fuel. Spacecraft are therefore aimed at the position the Moon will be in by the time the craft arrives. They navigate by the stars.

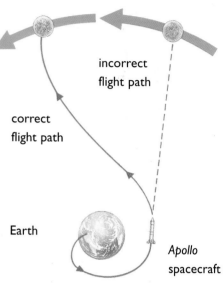

▲ **Moving targets**
This diagram shows two possible flight paths for an *Apollo* spacecraft. Aiming directly at the Moon does not allow for its movement as it orbits the Earth. The correct, efficient route compensates for the Moon's orbital movements by aiming ahead of its position at lift-off.

YOU WILL NEED

Moving target: string, ruler, scissors, masking tape, metal washer, book, small balls of paper.

Two-stage rocket: two paper or plastic cups, scissors, long balloon and pump, tape, round balloon.

Moving target

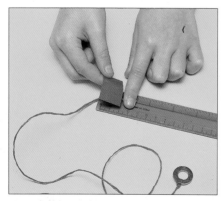

1 Measure 2ft of string with the ruler. Cut it off with scissors. Tape one end of the string to one end of the ruler. Tie a washer to the other end of the string.

2 Place the ruler on a table or box, with the string hanging over the edge. Weigh it down with a heavy book. Try hitting the washer by throwing small balls of paper at it.

3 Start the washer swinging, and try to hit it again with the paper balls. See how much more difficult it is to hit a moving target, like a spacecraft aiming at the moving Moon.

third stage powers
command/service module
(CSM) toward the Moon

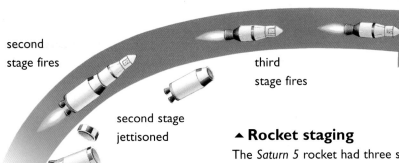

second
stage fires

third
stage fires

second stage
jettisoned

first stage
jettisoned

▲ Rocket staging

The *Saturn 5* rocket had three stages.
The first two powered the spacecraft up
through the atmosphere. The third
stage propelled it into orbit, and then
gave an extra push to send the craft
on its way to the Moon.

Two-stage rocket

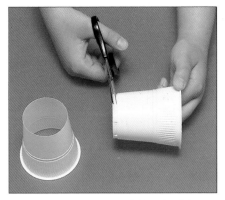

1 Using scissors, carefully cut the
bottoms out of the paper or plastic
cups. These will serve as the linking
collar between the two stages of the
balloon rocket.

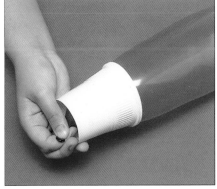

2 Partly blow up the long balloon
with the pump. Pull the neck of
the balloon through the paper or
plastic cups. This balloon will be your
two-stage rocket's second stage.

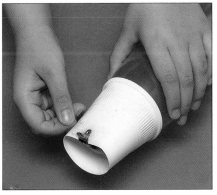

3 Fold the neck of the long balloon
over the side of the cups. Tape
the end of the neck of the balloon
to the cups to stop the air from
escaping, as shown.

4 Carefully push the round balloon
into the open end of the paper or
plastic cups, as shown. This balloon will
form the first stage of your two-stage
balloon rocket.

5 Blow up the round balloon, so that
it wedges the neck of the long
balloon in place inside the cups. Hold
the neck of the round balloon to
keep the air inside it.

Peel the tape off the
neck of the long balloon.
Hold the rocket as shown.
Let go of the round
balloon's neck. Air rushes
out, launching the first stage
of the rocket. It then falls
away, launching the second-
stage balloon.

Artificial gravity

Space travelers in orbit far away from Earth do not feel the pull of gravity. They feel weightless, as if they are forever falling. In a state of weightlessness, there is no up or down, because up and down are created by the force known as gravity. Even experienced pilots and astronauts sometimes feel uncomfortable and ill until they get used to being weightless. Weightlessness also has damaging effects on the human body. Future space stations and spacecraft designed for very long spaceflights may create artificial gravity to protect their occupants from the effects of weightlessness.

In this project, you can explore a theoretical method of creating artificial gravity that uses rotation by making a centrifuge. Moving objects tend to travel in straight lines. When you whirl around a ball attached to the end of a piece of string, it tries to fly off in a straight line, stopped only by the string. Inside a rotating spacecraft, the solid outer walls would stop astronauts flying off in straight lines. This would feel like the astronauts were being pushed down to the ground, just like the effect of gravity on Earth.

YOU WILL NEED

four thick card triangles (12 x 4 x 8¾in), dishwashing detergent bottle, tape, bradawl, wooden skewer, long rubber band, masking tape, three paper clips, pliers, thick card strip (20 x 2in), small bead, scissors, drinking straw, two small plastic cups, nonhardening modeling material, water, food coloring.

Make a centrifuge

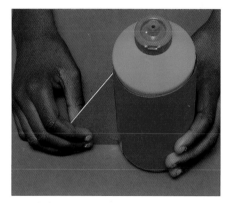

1 Take the four card triangles and tape them to the sides of the bottle, as shown. These will provide the dishwashing detergent centrifuge with a broad, stable base to stand on.

2 Using the bradawl, make a hole in the bottom of the detergent bottle. Push one end of the rubber band almost all the way into the hole using a wooden skewer.

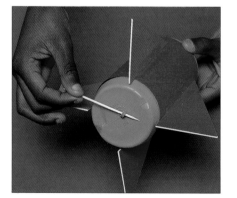

3 Pass the wooden skewer through the small loop of rubber band projecting from the hole, as shown. Leave an equal amount of skewer on either side of the bottle.

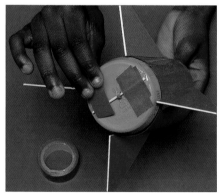

4 Take the masking tape and firmly secure the wooden skewer to the base of the detergent bottle. Make sure that the skewer is fixed so tightly that it cannot move.

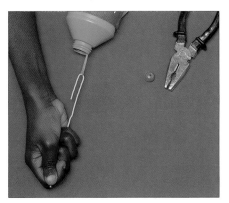

5 Straighten out one end of a paper clip with pliers. Dip the hooked end of the clip into the neck of the bottle. Catch the rubber band with the hook and pull it out.

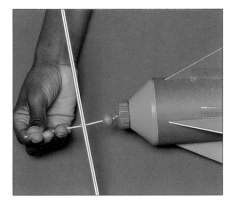

6 Using the bradawl, make a hole in the middle of the 20 x 2in card strip. Thread the end of the hooked paper clip through the bead. Then thread it through the hole in the card.

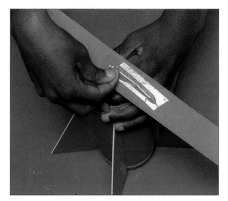

7 Carefully bend the end of the paper clip down onto the card strip. Using the tape, fix the end of the clip securely into place, as shown above.

8 Use the scissors to cut two short pieces of drinking straw. Each piece should measure 2in in length. Fix one piece to each end of the card strip with the tape.

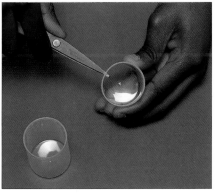

9 Take one of the small plastic cups. Carefully make a hole with the scissors on both sides of the cup near the top. Now make holes in the second cup in the same way.

Stick the centrifuge to a flat surface with modeling material. Fill the cups one-quarter full with water. Add food coloring to make the water show up clearly. Then turn the card strip until the rubber band is wound up. Let the strip go, and watch the cups as they spin around rapidly. The cups fly outward, but the water is held in place by the bases of the cups.

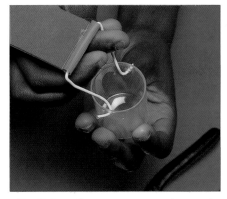

10 Straighten two paper clips with pliers. Thread a clip through each straw. Bend the ends of the clips into hooks using pliers. Thread the ends of the clips through the holes in the cups.

Working in Space

There is no gravity outside the pressurized crew compartment of a shuttle in Space. This makes work more difficult than on Earth. On Earth, gravity pulls us down to the ground. We can then use friction against the ground in order to move around. If a weightless astronaut pushes a handle in zero gravity, he or she would fly away in the opposite direction! This means that astronauts have to be anchored to something solid before doing any work. A spacesuit makes it even more difficult to move. The astronaut has to push against the suit to close a hand, or bend an arm or leg.

▲ **Working in a spacesuit**
Bulky spacesuits make working in Space difficult. Spacesuit designers are always trying to improve them. The more flexible a suit is, the less tiring it is to work in. This means that an astronaut can work outside for longer periods, a great help when they are making repairs.

Spacesuit gloves have thin rubber fingerpacks, so that astronauts can feel things through them, but their sense of touch is still very limited. The first project simulates the experience of working in a spacesuit by using rubber gloves, a bowl of water, and some nuts and bolts. Then make a robot arm like the shuttle's remote manipulator system (RMS), which is used to launch and retrieve satellites.

Working in Space

1 Take the nuts and bolts, and place them on a table. Now try picking them up and screwing them together. You should find this a very easy task to achieve!

2 Now try screwing the nuts and bolts together with the gloves on. This is more difficult, like trying to perform a delicate task on Earth wearing bulky spacesuit gloves.

3 Fill the bowl with water. Add the nuts and bolts. Try screwing them together with the gloves on. This is very difficult, like working in a spacesuit outside a spacecraft.

Make a robot arm

1 Use the ruler to measure three 11 x 2in card strips. Cut them out. Use a bradawl to make a hole 1in from the ends of each strip. Join the strips with split pins.

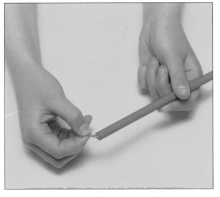

2 Take the hook and screw it into the end of the dowel. The dowel will be used to control the robot arm remotely, just as shuttle astronauts remotely operate the RMS.

3 Now carefully bend one of the paper clips into the shape of the letter S. To attach the paper clip, pass it through the hole in the end of the cardboard arm, as shown.

4 Take the modeling material and roll it into a ball about the size of a walnut. Then take the second paper clip and push it firmly into the ball, as shown.

Pass the hook on the dowel through the hole in the end of the cardboard arm. Move the dowel to operate the robot arm remotely. Try to pick up the ball using the S-shaped paper clip.

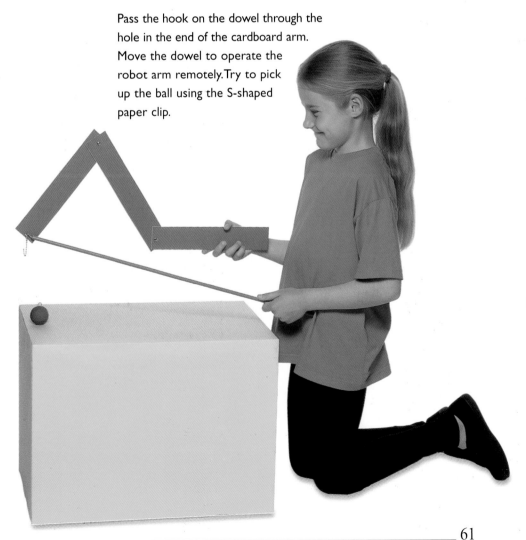

Glossary

A

aerodynamics The way in which objects move through the air.

aileron A moving flap on the trailing (rear) edge of the wing of an aircraft.

air pressure The force with which air presses on things. Changes in air pressure make air move and cause different weather conditions.

airfoil An object, shaped like a wing, that creates lift in the air.

B

bilge pumps The pumps found on ships and boats that are used to pump out water that has collected in the bottom of the hull and expel it back into the sea or river.

bow The front end of a ship.

brake A pad or disk that slows a moving surface down by pressing it.

brake van A carriage at the back of trains used in the mid-1800s. A guard riding in the brake van applied the brakes on instructions from the driver in the locomotive.

buoyancy The ability of an object to float in or on water.

C

camshaft A device that creates a regular, rocking movement, such as the opening and shutting of a valve on a car cylinder head.

capsize When a boat or vehicle that travels in water tips over completely.

cargo Goods carried in a ship or other vehicle.

compass An instrument containing a magnetized strip of metal, used for finding direction.

compressed air Air that has been squashed into a smaller volume than usual.

conductor A material through which heat or electricity can travel.

counterweight A weight used to balance out another weight.

coupling A connecting device that joins a locomotive to a carriage to make a train.

coupling rod A link that connects the driving wheels on both sides of a locomotive.

crankshaft An axle found on motor vehicles that has parts of it bent at right angles so that up-and-down motion can be turned into circular motion.

cross section The surface revealed when a solid object is sliced through, especially at right angles to its length.

cylinder A hollow or solid tube shape.

D

density A measure of how tightly the matter in a substance is packed together.

drag A force that acts in the opposite direction to motion and creates resistance.

driving wheel The wheel found on locomotives that turns in response to power generated from the steam engine.

E

effort The force applied to a lever or other machine to move a load.

elevator In aircraft, a movable flap on the tailplane or rear wing that causes the nose to rise or fall.

engine A device that uses energy in fuel to make movement.

escape velocity The minimum speed that a body must have to escape from the gravitational force of a planet.

F

ferry A boat that carries passengers and often cars across a river or a stretch of water.

force A push or a pull.

freight Goods transported by rail, road, sea or air.

freight train A train that carries goods rather than passengers.

G

gauge The width between the inside running edges of the rails of a train track. In the USA the gauge is 4ft 8½ in. In Britain and most of Europe it is 1,435mm.

gear A toothed wheel designed to interact with other toothed wheels to transfer motion.

locomotive An engine powered by steam, diesel or electricity that is used to pull the carriages of a train.

M
monorail A train that runs on a single rail.

N
navigation The skill of plotting a route for vehicles such as ships, aircraft or cars.

O
orbit In astronomy, the curved path followed by a planet or other body around another planet or body.

P
piston A cylindrical device that moves up and down inside a cylinder in response to the application and release of pressure from liquid or gas.

pivot A central point around which something revolves, balances or sways.

points Rails at a fork in the track, which can move to guide a locomotive on to the desired track.

propellant The fuel or force that causes something to go forward, such as the fuel in a rocket.

propeller A device, with blades, that rotate to provide thrust for a vehicle such as a ship or plane.

prototype The first working model of a machine from a specific design.

R
rolling stock Any vehicles, such as locomotives, carriages and wagons, that operate on railroads.

rudder A device found on ships and airplanes, used to control the direction of travel.

S
Solar system The family of planets, moons and other bodies that orbit around the Sun.

steam traction Pulling movement achieved through the conversion of water to steam.

streamlined A shape that moves through air or water in the most efficient manner, with the least resistance from drag or friction.

T
thrust The force that pushes something such as an aircraft forwards.

turbine A propeller-like device driven by fast-moving gas currents, wind, or water.

turbulence Air or water movement that consists of eddies in random directions, with no smooth flow.

U
underframe The frame that supports the bodywork of a car or railroad train.

upthrust The force that makes a ship float or an aircraft take off.

W
waterwheel A simple, water-driven turbine used to drive machinery.

H
hovercraft A vehicle that is able to move over land or water on a cushion of air.

hull The frame or body of a ship or aircraft.

hydrofoil A boat with wing-like 'foils' under the hull, which raise it out of the water as it goes faster.

I
insulate To cover or protect something to reduce the amount of heat or electricity entering and/or leaving it.

J
jet engine A type of engine that propels a vehicle, such as a car or a plane, by the the forceful expulsion of hot gases.

jet propulsion Movement as a reaction to a jet of fluid or gas.

L
leading wheel The wheel at the front of a locomotive.

lift The force generated by air moving over an airfoil, because of its shape, that counters the force of gravity and keeps a flying object in the air.

load The weight moved by a lever or other machine.

Index